CONTENTS

Introduction

An international conference titled *People, Wildlife and Hunting: Emerging Conservation Paradigms* convened in Edmonton, Alberta, on October 24 – 26, 2004. The purpose of the conference was to bring together people sharing a common interest or involvement in conservation hunting. The Edmonton conference focused attention more particularly (but not exclusively) upon conservation hunting programs operating in the Canadian North. Participants included hunters, outfitters, wildlife managers, community representatives, conservationists, and researchers from the three Canadian northern territories, several Canadian provinces and from overseas (Australia, Hungary, Russia, the United Kingdom and the U.S.A).

One particular objective of the conference was to explore the relationship linking trophy hunting, wildlife conservation and community sustainability in rural areas, using the extensive experiences gained in northern Canada where such hunting programs are generally well-received in the communities and by the responsible wildlife management agencies. Our common purpose in convening this meeting was to move toward a better understanding of what constitutes conservation hunting best practices.

The idea for such a conference originated at a well-attended symposium on conservation hunting held in December 2003 during the 3rd International Wildlife Management Congress meeting in Christchurch, New Zealand. Following the Christchurch symposium, those who had presented papers agreed to continue and expand discussion of this topic. In view of the recognized importance of hunting to large-mammal management and community sustainability in many rural areas of Canada, and more especially in the Canadian North, the Canadian Circumpolar Institute (CCI) and the Alberta Cooperative Conservation Research Unit (ACCRU) at the University of Alberta organized the *People, Wildlife and Hunting Conference*. The conference organizing committee consisted of Milton Freeman (representing CCI) and Lee Foote and Bob Hudson (representing

ACCRU). The list of sponsors and others who assisted the conference organizers is provided below.

The Edmonton conference included individual papers, two panel discussions, four small-group discussions, a guided fieldtrip to Elk Island National Park, and a post-conference workshop to discuss conference outcomes and useful follow-up initiatives. This report contains short summaries of the papers and discussions held during the conference, together with the conference program and participants' contact information.

Acknowledgements

The organizers wish to thank the following conference sponsors for financial support:

Alberta Conservation Association
Alberta Professional Outfitters' Society – Legacy Fund
Protected Areas Strategy, Government of the Northwest Territories
Safari Club International Foundation
Safari Club International – Northern Alberta Chapter
University of Alberta Conference Fund

We are grateful to Nunavut Tunngavik Inc. for arranging a meeting of Nunavut wildlife officials in Edmonton in order to facilitate their participation in the *People, Wildlife and Hunting* conference.

Special thanks to Elaine Maloney, Cindy Mason, and Mike Salomons of the Canadian Circumpolar Institute, Shevenell Mullen and Michael Fisher, University of Alberta, for assistance with the conference and the conference report. Superintendent Robert Sheldon and Wes Olson of Parks Canada kindly arranged and hosted an informative and enjoyable visit to Elk Island National Park. Fraser Gallop of Onware Software Corporation provided website and associated services. We are also grateful to Amy Csobot and her staff at Daltons' Conference Centre and the staff at the Greenwood Inn for their courteous and efficient assistance before and during the conference.

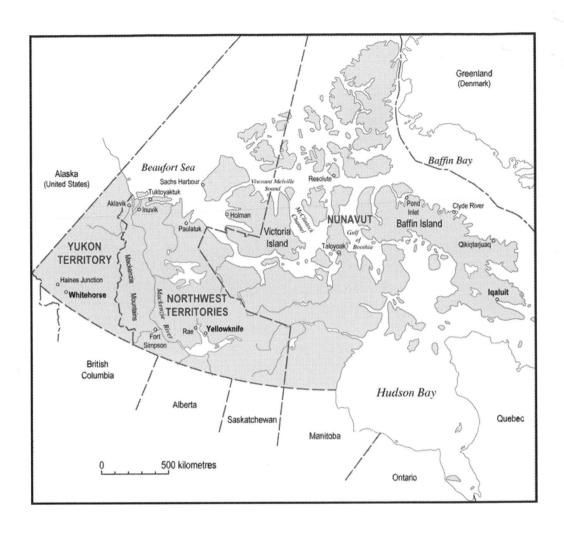

Greenland
(Denmark)

Baffin Bay

Beaufort Sea

Alaska
(United States)

Sachs Harbour

Resolute

Tuktoyaktuk

Viscount Melville
Sound

Aklavik

Isuvik

Holman

Pond
Inlet

Clyde River

Paulatuk

NUNAVUT

Baffin Island

YUKON
TERRITORY

Victoria
Island

Gulf
of
Boothia

Qikiqtarjuaq

Taloyoak

Haines Junction

Mackenzie

Whitehorse

NORTHWEST
TERRITORIES

Iqaluit

Mountains

Rae

Yellowknife

Fort
Simpson

Mackenzie River

British
Columbia

Hudson Bay

Alberta

Quebec

Saskatchewan

Manitoba

0   500 kilometres

Ontario

A Framework Proposal for Conservation-Hunting Best Practices

William A. Wall
Conservation Biologist
Purceville, Virginia 20132, USA

Introduction

Since 1998, there has been growing interest from the international conservation community to develop hunting program 'standards.' To advance this process, I propose here a draft set of 'Best Practices' for conservation-hunting programs. These 'Best Practices' are intended to provide a broad framework for governments, resource managers, local communities, hunters and other interested stakeholders to consider when discussing or implementing conservation-hunting programs.

A conservation-hunting program is one that contributes to the short and long-term viability of a species by generating incentives, management regimes, and/or sources of funds to:

- support maintenance, and if required, restoration of associated habitats and ecosystems;

- develop and implement the means for effective monitoring of the targeted population;

- develop and implement a regulatory framework;

- assure maintenance of genetic diversity within and among populations of the species;

- ensure that other intensive uses of habitats, such as, e.g., grazing of domestic livestock or industrial development, are compatible with the maintenance of wildlife populations.

Trophy Hunting

Trophy hunting is a specialized form of sport hunting that provides an excellent basis for conservation-hunting programs because:

- trophy hunters take very few animals that meet specific criteria (e.g., usually large-size antlers or horns normally associated with older males);

- sustainable trophy hunting requires populations having a healthy demographic structure, maintained in habitats of sufficient quality for the population to be productive, and with control over such negative impacts as poaching;

- only a limited number of people engage in trophy hunting and as each trophy hunter requires little enabling infrastructure, there is little direct environmental impact affecting habitat, wildlife populations or local societies and their institutions;

- trophy hunters usually travel some distance from the normal hunting grounds of subsistence or other recreational hunters, thus distributing hunters to less frequented rural areas of the world;

- trophy hunters place high economic value on their pursuits, so that properly managed programs increase the economic benefits flowing from wildlife use to rural peoples;

- trophy hunting is easily monitored and controlled, because trophy hunters are licensed to hunt and typically require the services of licensed guides.

Conserving Biodiversity

There is a realization among conservationists (reflected in recent international environmental conventions and accords) that sustainable use of natural resources is an important means for conserving biodiversity. As the world's protected areas are insufficient to adequately conserve global biodiversity, achieving conservation of biodiversity depends on augmenting those conservation strategies by using natural resources in a manner that achieves a greater degree of *in-situ* conservation. In many areas, sport and trophy hunting, when conducted under appropriate controls and utilizing well-informed management, are the least intrusive programs and can provide enhanced economic and political support for *in-situ* conservation.

Essential Elements for Effective Conservation Hunting
Conservation-hunting programs will be enhanced if:

- social and economic incentives ensure meaningful involvement of indigenous and local communities in the program;

- effective monitoring provides critical feedback on the success or failure of the program in the context of an adaptive management approach;

- mechanisms are in place to monitor and adjust (if required) quotas or other permit conditions, including temporarily suspending hunting in order to sustain the viability of the target population;

- the program contributes to the short- and long-term viability of the target species by maintaining population segments of sufficient size and demographic structures to allow normal breeding behavior to continue;

- the program ensures that sufficient areas and quality of habitat exist to sustain productive populations;

- hunting quotas take account of unforeseen factors and unpredictable events (e.g., disease outbreaks, other natural disasters);

- the program generates and contributes funds to support management activities including monitoring and program implementation.

Criteria for Conservation-Hunting Programs
All management programs suffer from limited information. However, basic information is required for, and can be improved by, conservation-hunting programs. Such information includes that needed to establish an initial quota for a hunting program as well as that required to support an adaptive management program. It is also desirable at the outset to plan to gather information from the hunting program that may support additional relevant research.

Minimum information necessary to set initial hunting quotas includes a general knowledge of the life history and biology of the species, including potentially limiting factors, expected reproductive rates, and some appreciation of population status of the species throughout its geographic range.

In relation to the population where the conservation-hunting program is operating more especially, information on past harvest estimates (if any exits), including the number and sex of animals harvested is also important, as is survey data providing the estimated number of adult males, females and juveniles in the local population. An understanding of threats associated with human-induced factors in the program area, including habitat loss, subsistence use, alternative human uses for habitats (e.g., livestock grazing), and expected future trends in these and other factors should be obtained.

Adaptive management aims to continually improve program outcomes by refining the above-mentioned management-relevant information. Of particular interest and importance are trends of relative density and demographic structure of hunted populations (obtained directly from the hunted animals), periodic census and incidental observations. Harvest information includes numbers harvested by sex, age, size classes of trophies, and reproductive status of females. Estimates of productivity trends through time are based on both periodic census and annual harvest information (such as hunt-success rates).

Additional research, conducted with funds and expertise outside the hunting program, can provide such useful information as genetic variation within and among populations, the influence of disease on target species and overall ecosystem health, demographic structure and population productivity associated with different quality habitats, and environmental factors affecting target populations. Related to these demographic concerns are the relationships among predators, prey and competitor populations, and estimates of habitat quantity and quality and changes through time.

Social and Economic Environment

Quite apart from biological considerations, successful conservation-hunting programs involve a number of social and economic factors, including, e.g., marketing and service arrangements, economic returns sufficient to ensure the viability of the activity and provision of benefits to local communities or landowners, and mechanisms to ensure local community involvement.

Employment and access payments may not be the only benefits participating communities or landowners derive from conservation-hunting programs. 'Opportunity costs' must be understood within an appropriate social and cultural context, such that the focus of concern becomes wildlife and local people, never wildlife or local people. It may be necessary to consider factors such as crop damage, livestock predation, and the danger wildlife poses to humans when calculating community costs.

When conservation-hunting programs successfully involve local communities, some degree of training in new skills and support for new functions on the part of rural people may be required. Participation can be encouraged and solicited in meaningful ways. To be successful, such programs require significant community involvement in planning, decision-making, implementation, and evaluation activities.

Control and Empowerment Legislation

Specific legislation and administrative arrangements pertaining to conservation hunting are required to develop and implement hunting quotas, seasons, approved methods, and other such limitations as are deemed necessary to regulate these programs. It may be necessary to legislate the establishment of management and refuge areas to sustain the quality and quantity of necessary habitats, and mechanisms by which payments from license and trophy fees can support development and implementation of wildlife conservation/management plans and enforcement measures. Of special importance are legislation and policies that ensure local communities and/or individuals are meaningful partners in collaborative or co-management arrangements and otherwise derive benefit from conservation-hunting programs.

Accountability, Enforcement, and Incentives

While centralized law enforcement agencies can be effective in averting some illegal loss of wildlife, limitations in the number of enforcement officials (and in some regions, the danger of confronting armed poachers) may detract from the effectiveness of enforcement measures. Furthermore, the willingness of some hunters to pay high costs to obtain rare or challenging trophy animals may subvert any wildlife management program. Consequently, enforcement requires both incentives and sanctions to deter illegal hunting and smuggling.

Those closest to the wildlife are important allies in detecting hunting abuses and enforcing regulations. Empowering communities, by providing culturally-appropriate incentives to local individuals and institutions, is critical to the success of any regulatory enforcement approach.

Conclusions

The above-mentioned measures and capacities require administrative support and adequate funding if the management programs are to succeed. This may require new structures for establishing, training and equipping conservation agencies and communities to administer and enforce applicable laws, regulations and programs for the sustainable use of wild species. It may also require integrating management activities with the work of other government agencies, particularly those involved with regulating land use, e.g., departments of economic development, forestry, tourism and recreation, municipal/local government affairs, etc.

Incentives that aim to provide long-term economic benefits by creating stable business-operating climates for landowners, communities, or hunting concession holders will encourage these partners to invest in equitable wildlife management arrangements in specific hunting areas. Such business considerations help assure safeguards against overexploitation or unregulated killing of wildlife. Such incentives will include any programs that reinforce local social and cultural institutions, practices, or customs that act as functional equivalents to government actions in limiting access or otherwise controlling the unsustainable use of wildlife.

Conservation and Hunting in Northern Regions: Community-Based Hunting as a Conservation Tool

Peter J. Ewins
Arctic Conservation Director
WWF-Canada, Toronto

Introduction

World Wildlife Fund—Canada (WWF) has supported many community-based and applied conservation research projects in Canada's northern territories over the past 30 years. In conjunction with various technical, policy and advocacy initiatives, our overall aim in Canada's North is to help conserve natural ecosystems with wildlife and people in healthy condition, while we still have the opportunity.

WWF-Canada is part of the WWF global network, comprising over 5 million members and active conservation projects in over 100 countries. WWF's global mission is *"To stop the degradation of the planet's natural environment and to build a future in which humans live in harmony with nature."*

A central pillar of WWF's work is the concept of sustainability for the long-term, or Sustainable Development (defined as 'development that meets the needs of the present without compromising the ability of future generations to meet their own needs'). We believe that any well-balanced approach to regional development must place equal emphasis on economic, social and environmental factors. This approach is very similar to that traditionally taken to decision-making by most indigenous peoples' groups. For example, Canada's Inuvialuit have a traditional saying: 'If we look after our resources, our resources will always look after us.'

Today, indigenous peoples inhabit nearly 20 percent of our planet. Most of these inhabited areas are essentially still in their natural state, with intact ecosystems rich in native biodiversity. This makes indigenous peoples one of the most important groups of stewards of the world's biodiversity. In many regions, including most northern countries, WWF works closely with local people to achieve large-scale conservation goals for natural habitats and wildlife species. This includes engagement with community-based, well-monitored and well-managed wildlife and natural resource management programs (some of which involve hunting), which generate much needed revenue for communities.

WWF believes that well-managed hunting by local people in these northern regions constitutes a very important conservation tool, whereby future generations will continue to value highly these natural areas for the wildlife populations they support. In the face of escalating industrial development pressures in many northern regions, this is a time-limited opportunity to get the balance of development and conservation right.

Recognising a number of past experiences with over-harvesting of wildlife populations in northern regions, WWF commissioned a circumarctic review of wildlife species utilization which examined the use of wildlife in the eight Arctic countries in relation to 15 guidelines developed globally for wild species' (commercial) use. In general, we found that the guidelines developed for commercial consumptive use of wild species globally were applicable in arctic situations for both commercial and more subsistence-oriented use. Therefore, these reviews and the guidelines themselves are very useful background and tools for those involved with planning and decision-making in northern areas, to ensure that wildlife populations and hunting can persist in the long-term.

This paper uses a current example—in the Mackenzie Valley of Canada's Northwest Territories—to illustrate the need for, and progress to date with, a very different conservation-based approach to industrial development in northern regions. With rapid acceleration of natural gas exploration and development in northwestern Canada, the proposed $7 Billion Mackenzie Gas Pipeline looks set to trigger a major era of industrial development in the region. The Mackenzie Valley Protected Areas Strategy Action Plan 2004 to 2009, is now being implemented to establish an extensive network of special cultural and ecological areas in the region before completion of this major pipeline development. Most of these special natural areas are known to be key hunting areas for Dene and Inuvialuit people (and hence areas of high cultural, spiritual and historic values). The Aboriginal inhabitants of the region, while welcoming responsible economic development, also insist on being able to continue their traditional hunting, trapping and fishing practices.

The Consumptive Use of Wild Species in the Arctic: Challenges and Opportunities for Ecological Sustainability

The hunting of wild species is the most common, and most extensive, form of natural resource use across all the regions and peoples of the Arctic. But these same regions also hold globally significant deposits of non-renewable resources—oil, gas, coal, methane hydrates, metals, gems, etc. Getting the right balance of economic development and resource conservation is a major challenge and priority for northern peoples, governments, industry and conservation groups alike. No longer can society accept the old paradigms of industrial development, where resource riches were exploited as rapidly as possible with little regard for either northern peoples, wildlife, or any comprehensive long-term planning for economic, cultural, or environmental values.

Based on the extensive reviews and analyses carried out on behalf of WWF in the 1990s, the following 15 guidelines for the sustainable use of wild species were found to be broadly applicable in arctic situations. Provided such guidelines are adhered to, we believe that hunting can constitute an important wildlife management and conservation tool, particularly in the face of rapid northern industrial expansion, thus enabling wildlife resources use to be continued in a sustainable way for the long-term. These guidelines state that:

- Wild species have intrinsic worth and nourish human cultural and spiritual values that should balance the influence of economic forces in nature conservation.

- Consumptive use should be promoted only where it is likely to create conservation benefit.

- A goal of any consumptive use program should be to maintain current and future options by maintaining biodiversity and avoiding irreversible ecosystem changes.

- Natural ecological fluctuations and processes and the life histories of organisms should provide the blueprint according to which we design consumptive use programs.

- Adaptive management is required to cope with uncertainty in both ecological and socio-economic systems.

- Knowledge and skills from local user groups and traditional resource management systems should be integrated with knowledge from scientific research to improve design and monitoring of consumptive use programs.

- Revenues from consumptive use should be sufficient and distributed in such a way as to cover the costs of ecologically sustainable use and to create incentives for the conservation of biodiversity and natural ecosystems, but consumptive use should not be expected to carry the full costs.

- Diversified economic benefits from biodiversity and natural ecosystems, secured in part by getting those who profit from biodiversity-based values to pay their fair share, should be promoted.

- To make natural ecosystems competitive with alternative uses of land and water, some biodiversity may need to be sacrificed.

- Benchmarks of biodiversity and ecosystem integrity should be developed and used to set conservation goals, to define acceptable limits of change due to consumptive use, and to provide a standard against which to monitor change.

- Ecological and socio-economic subsidies will often be required to make the transition toward sustainability.

- Management of wild species should be balanced between assigning resource tenure and management responsibility to the lowest level commensurate with the scale of resource use and regulation by broader authorities for the public good.

- The full value of biodiversity and ecosystem services should be reflected in decision-making about management of the natural ecosystem.

- Market demand should be more effectively used as a tool to promote better management.

- Better national and international coordination and action are required to improve the sustainability of consumptive use as a conservation tool, and to mitigate the negative impacts of consumptive use on biodiversity.

Putting 'Conservation First' in the Mackenzie Valley, Northwest Territories

In the Mackenzie Valley, Aboriginal peoples have, for thousands of years, depended totally on the land, freshwater and bountiful wildlife resources. These northern boreal forest and tundra regions are among the most extensive remaining natural ecosystems on the planet inhabited by humans. Successful conservation of these ecosystems and the wildlife populations they support is a major priority both for local people and for WWF. Beneath the ground in the Mackenzie basin lies the northern parts of the Western Canada Sedimentary Basin, one of the continent's largest deposits of fossil fuel reserves, notably oil, tar sands, methane hydrates, and natural gas.

In the 1970s, Canada's largest ever Royal Commission (the Berger Inquiry) reflected the strong views of NWT residents and placed a moratorium on major expansion of oil and gas developments pending settlement of Aboriginal land claims. Today, nearly all those land claims in the region are settled, and the claims' beneficiaries support the development of natural gas reserves and the proposed Mackenzie Gas Pipeline provided that these industrial developments should only take place in a way that allows for adequate conservation of cultural and environmental values. Thus Aboriginal peoples insist that hunting, trapping and fishing traditions, sources of clean water, and key cultural and wildlife areas all continue to be adequately protected.

Although subsistence hunting has declined in the NWT over recent decades, a majority of NWT residents in smaller communities are still very active on the land, engaging in hunting, fishing, and trapping. Sport hunting for big game species, usually guided by local outfitters, appears to be increasing in the NWT, and this will likely continue with increasing industrial presence in the region (see Table 1).

Table 1. Key statistics and trends of NWT hunting, fishing and trapping (source: NWT Biodiversity Action Plan, 2004)

• 44% of NWT adults hunt and fish (stable % over the past 20 years).
• 3% decline in non-native residents' hunting licenses, over past 10 years.
• Banks Island muskox harvest is the largest NWT commercial harvest (peak of 2,031 taken in 1991, from a muskox population of ca. 65,000).
• Commercial fisheries in steady decline (e.g., Great Slave Lake fishery).
• Outfitted big game hunts increasing (e.g., 15% per year increase in the case of barren-ground caribou hunts).
• 20-year decline in trapping (2,775 sold furs in 1981, but only 755 in 2003).
• 75% of NWT residents harvesting (in communities with fewer than 1,000 residents).

At the forefront of these new industrial opportunities, the community-based NWT Protected Areas Strategy (PAS) (http://www.gov.nt.ca/RWED/pas/), and the PAS Action Plan, 2004-2009 (http://ww.wwf.ca), have been developed cooperatively by the regional Aboriginal organizations, governments, environmental organizations, and industry, to ensure that an adequate network of special natural areas are identified and reserved prior to completion of this major gas pipeline from the Mackenzie Delta south to the continental pipeline network. Many of these extensive special natural areas will be protected from industrial development via this community-based PAS process.

In line with Aboriginal traditional approaches, WWF calls this new precautionary approach the 'Conservation First' principle. We believe that only in this way will society have a reasonable chance of ensuring that sufficient intact natural habitat is available to allow wildlife populations, and the people who continue to depend upon them, to flourish in the long-term.

Conclusion

If society values sustainable hunting, trapping and fishing of wild species in northern regions, two key things must happen:

- Sufficient intact natural habitat must be safeguarded while the opportunity to do so still exists, that is to say, ahead of industrial developments;

- Utilisation of wildlife populations must follow key principles and guidelines, so that lessons learned from past mistakes in these regions, and elsewhere in the world, will not be repeated.

The challenge in establishing a new paradigm for conservation and development in the North is to use the tools we already have. If we are to achieve 'Sustainable Development' goals, we must clearly adopt the lessons learned from past mistakes from whatever cause, including over-hunting.

The past 'development first' approach to habitat use and management (often to the exclusion of conservation/traditional community values) must be replaced by a 'conservation first' approach, so that wildlife populations remain healthy enough to be hunted sustainably in the long-term.

Acknowledgements

I am grateful to Dr. Susan Lieberman (WWF-International) and Arlin Hackman (WWF-Canada) for comments on a previous draft of this manuscript, and to WWF-Canada's supporters who enabled me to participate in this conference.

Sports Hunting in the Western Canadian Arctic

James Pokiak
Ookpik Tours and Adventures
Tuktoyaktuk, Northwest Territories

My name is James Pokiak and I live in Tuktoyaktuk in the Northwest Territories. I would like to thank the organizers for asking me to speak about sports hunting at this conference.

Talking about conservation, I want to tell you what my Dad said to me and my brothers. By the time we were old enough to hunt and trap, my Dad was no longer able to take us out hunting, but he always said that if you look after the lands and the animals and the environment, then the land and the animals would look after you.

I run an outfitter/guiding operation in Tuktoyaktuk (also called Tuk in the region) which is located along the arctic coast. I book hunts for polar bear, muskox, central barren-ground grizzly bear and central barren-ground caribou. I have been involved in big game guiding since the early 1980s, first as a guide, then in the mid 1990s as a booking agent and guide, and now owning my own outfitting business. Presently there are six outfitters for sports hunting operating in Tuk. These six outfitters have access to 13 polar bear tags, 25 muskox tags, 6 grizzly bear tags and about 80 caribou tags for bookings.

The number of polar bears that may be harvested have been set for years by the co-management bodies run through the Northwest Territories' Department of Renewable Resources and the Inuvialuit Land Claims organization. Studies of the population will continue to dictate the quota for polar bears. There is not too much concern from the local hunters over the number of tags set aside for sports hunting polar bears.

Similarly, the number of tags set aside for sports hunting muskox and central barren-ground caribou have not caused a lot of dissent.

Muskox are not hunted much in our area for subsistence. Muskox are found about 130 km from our community, whereas the caribou are generally much closer to the town. This past year, all of Tuk's muskox tags were allotted to the outfitters for sports hunting. The local hunters do not need caribou tags for subsistence hunting. So Tuk's caribou tags are divided between the outfitters and commercial tags for the sale of meat to non-aboriginals.

The greatest area of concern for the subsistence hunters and the outfitters is over central barren-ground grizzly hunts. In the past three or four years, there seem to be more nuisance or problem bears getting into camps and wrecking cabins, and as well it seems they are becoming more daring in the presence of humans. Presently, half the 12 tags allotted for harvesting grizzly bears are assigned for sports hunting. The remaining six tags have to cover local subsistence hunters as well as kills of nuisance bears. The quota of grizzly bear tags has been increased by three just this season, but no decision has been made as to whether outfitters or local hunters will have access to them.

There have been attempts to hold guide-training courses, but the cost of the program has limited the number of communities where it has been presented.

Some of the challenges for big game outfitters to think about are:

1. How to encourage youth and young adults to spend extended periods of time out on the land so as they learn traditional hunting skills and understand traditional knowledge required to take clients safely on hunts on the arctic sea-ice and inland for sports hunting.
2. How climate changes are going to affect the animal populations and their habitat. Will animals' migration routes or time of migration change? Will the species' population numbers increase or decrease?
3. How will tags be distributed among the subsistence hunters and outfitters?

4. Thinking about mad cow disease, what other diseases may impede the hunting and transportation of trophies across borders?

Panel Discussion: Economics, Values, and Equitable Management

Sylvia Birkholz
Alberta Department of Sustainable Resource Development
Naomi Krogman
Department of Rural Economy, University of Alberta
Marty Luckert
Department of Rural Economy, University of Alberta
Kelly Semple
Hunting for Tomorrow Foundation

Statistical Profile of Hunting in Alberta

In the most recent years in Alberta, sale of hunting licenses have generated between $9.5–$9.8 Million annually. These revenues are divided between the Alberta Conservation Association (41 percent), the Alberta Professional Outfitters' Association (2 percent), general government revenues (36 percent), with the remainder used to operate the government's hunting license and statistical service. About 75 percent of hunting licenses are purchased by Alberta residents, and the remainder by non-residents (other Canadians and foreign hunters). The total number of hunters has remained fairly constant over the past six years, numbering between 90,000 –100,000 per year. 71 percent of hunters are classed as 'regular or avid hunters' (purchasing 3 or 4 licenses respectively over the last four years), and 16 percent are new hunters.

Outfitters, Outreach, and Hunters' Success

Non-resident hunters require the services of a registered outfitter to hunt in Alberta. With over 420 licensed outfitters and more than 90 percent of these outfitters' clients coming from outside of Alberta, the Alberta Professional Outfitters' Society (APOS) represents this sector of the provincial tourism industry. APOS has established a Legacy Fund for the purpose of protecting Alberta's hunting heritage and to ensure some of the revenues generated through hunting are channeled back to benefit all Albertans. Recent data indicated that in 2001 for example, hunters and the hunting industry in Alberta generated revenues of about $118 Million and 1,428 permanent jobs. The APOS Legacy Fund has allocated $288,000 to 34 projects, including wildlife inventories, school field-studies programs, bear awareness and relocation programs, and a mentorship program for first-time hunters. In 2001, non-resident hunters' success rates ranged from highs of 88 and 81 percent (for antelope and black bear hunts, respectively), 60 percent (for moose), in the 40 percent range (for white-tailed deer and mountain sheep), and 22 percent (for elk). Success rates for resident hunters are lower, ranging from 71 percent for antelope, down to 8 percent for elk.

Deriving Benefits from Hunting

From an economic perspective, in seeking how people or societies derive benefit from hunting, two factors in particular are important: *values* and *property rights*. People ascribe either *anthropocentric* or *ecocentric* values to wildlife. Anthropocentric values include, e.g., the pleasure or psychic/spiritual enrichment that comes from seeing, contemplating, or hunting animals. Ecocentric values include the importance ascribed to the perceived place of wildlife in maintaining 'the balance of nature' or ecosystem integrity. Anthropocentric values may be either passive use values (ascribed to rare or unseen species) or use values—which may be of a consumptive (hunting, harvesting) or non-consumptive (wildlife-viewing or photographing) nature.

Property Rights and Hunting Benefits

When considering the role of property rights in determining wildlife-derived benefits, there may be a number of different values influencing the outcome. These values in turn may be influenced by prevailing social conditions, including, e.g., who has access to wildlife, and should wildlife be sold or otherwise commercialized. Other questions include: what types of property-right structures enhance the value of wildlife, and what incentives can be created to maintain or enhance this value.

However, in seeking answers, determining the best form of property rights arrangements is complicated by the large variety of values that wildlife possesses under differing socially-derived circumstances. Additionally, there exist a large number of potential combinations of property-right arrangements to choose from, and although wildlife market failures are not uncommon, market situations may nevertheless provide useful management incentives.

Steps Toward Increasing Community Involvement in Wildlife Management

Wildlife management decision-making in different jurisdictions ranges from full centralized (state) control over management decisions, through various shared-control arrangements, to full stakeholder (including user-community) control. The degree of involvement of stakeholders in management decision-making may range from simple consultation, through various degrees of shared authority and responsibility (i.e., co-management), to exclusive management authority and responsibility being fully devolved to the local-community level.

Following Fikret Berkes' (1994) study, the following stages may be encountered on the road to co-management. These stages usually start with the beginning stage of *informing* (where the community is informed of decisions already made), through *consultation* (where community input is heard), *co-operation* (the usefulness of community input is acknowledged), *communication* (information exchanged and local concerns invited to be aired), to establishing *advisory committees* (common objectives and joint action agreed upon), followed by *management boards* (community participation in agenda setting) until, finally, *partnerships and community control* (institutionalized joint management decision-making) is achieved.

Exploitation and Conservation: Lessons from Southern Africa

Jon Hutton
Chair, IUCN-Sustainable Use Specialist Group
Cambridge, U.K.

Introduction

The exploitation of wild species is seen by many industrialised societies as a 'primitive' activity which many at the margins of the environmental community consider both unnecessary and immoral. David Favre, of the Animal Legal Defence Fund, expresses these points in the following way:

> *That a particular use of wildlife may be biologically and ecologically sustainable does not mean that it is ethically acceptable. Elephants are not turnips...To kill elephants for the sole purpose of selling their body parts like ivory is unacceptable.*

Furthermore, the harvesting of wild species for commercial purposes makes some conservationists very nervous indeed, and the unsophisticated response to this experience is the common assertion that markets are bad for conservation and international markets are worse.

What is promoted as an alternative is *preservation*, the hands-off management of nature.

At this point, let us turn to southern Africa where we can examine very quickly how effective more than a hundred years of preservationist conservation strategies have been.

Southern African Conservation—Reversing Historical Mistakes

Colonial governments will be remembered for their two-pronged approach to conservation in Africa: they created protected areas across the landscape, often evicting those who were living on the land, and they made laws prohibiting the use of many wild species by rural African people. Although the role of colonialism is subject to considerable debate, I think that there is little doubt that, in southern Africa at least, reliance on these twin strategies severed the link between African communities and wildlife, setting the scene for contemporary conservation problems—problems which have been exacerbated by the region's history of severe racial inequity.

In the absence of meaningful industrialisation, southern Africa's population and its hunger for land have grown, while rural poverty remains endemic. Protected areas are under pressure because they are seen by rural people as under-used and elitist, and also because they harbour dangerous wild animals that do not respect boundaries between different land types, however distinct they are on a map. As a result, these areas are increasingly being fenced, ostensibly to keep animals in, but without doubt, at least part of the agenda is to keep people and their cattle out. The countryside is polarised: elephants and lions have right of way in protected areas, but give way *absolutely* to man outside. Giving way increasingly means being eradicated.

This ecological apartheid, which is very easily seen from the air, relies on strict policing. Africa's rural people, who once lived off wildlife for which they often had traditional rules of access and management, are forbidden from using wildlife, and those who continue to do so are outlawed as poachers and accordingly harassed and hounded as criminals. This type of protection, which operates against the will of the people is doomed to failure in many, if not most, circumstances.

Africa's rural poor rely on natural resources for their survival and cannot easily be separated from wildlife. The levels of poverty experienced by many communities make bush meat the only affordable source of protein. The alternative to using wildlife is, commonly, severe malnutrition. And despite the law, latter-day Robin Hoods continue to use wildlife on a daily basis. The real effect of laws has not been to stop use, but to drive it 'underground,' making wildlife a free-for-all open-access resource. Traditional *sustainable use* has been replaced by institutionalised *abuse*.

As a result of preservationist approaches—which have been applied in a socio-economic vacuum—parks and other areas protected for wildlife are often under severe pressure in southern Africa. Other parts of the continent are littered with protected areas which exist only on maps and in the memories of old game rangers. As soon as there is the slightest excuse or opportunity, rural people have wasted no time in helping themselves to park resources, and that often includes the land itself.

At the same time, even where there are thriving tourism industries, African governments are failing to invest in parks and wildlife. Throughout the continent, budgets for protected area management have fallen steadily in real terms over the last decade, and with the many structural readjustment programs going on, this rate of fall appears to have increased. It is naive to think that this trend will be easily reversed, for the rural African voter simply has little or no sympathy for wildlife and the areas set aside for it to live in.

But this is far from the end of the story. Debarred from using wildlife legally, Africans have no alternative but to turn to domestic livestock and crops for their survival—even on the most miserable rural lands. This is the tragedy of the cow and the plough. Much of southern Africa is arid or semi-arid and far from suitable for agriculture. Despite this, more and more marginal land is being cleared, settled and cultivated. Wild land is disappearing simply because its wildlife products cannot compete with subsistence agriculture on an economic basis. Where cash crops are concerned, the situation is even worse. Huge tracts of land have been irreversibly degraded by inappropriate use. It is no exaggeration to describe this destruction of land and loss of productivity as southern Africa's greatest environmental problem.

As far as wildlife is concerned, settlement and agriculture turn the ratchet of extinction another notch. When there is cultivation, wildlife is not a cost-neutral package—more often than not it represents a major cost to rural people. Animals commonly destroy growing crops and foodstores, and loss of human life is all too common. The solution is inevitable. The wildlife has to go.

There is one final irony. While land is being degraded outside national parks, land inside the parks often fares little better. We tend to assume that parks are ecological nirvana, but sadly this is increasingly far from the truth. In particular, elephants do not magically maintain static numbers. Unless held back by the hand of man they increase, and ultimately are responsible, at least in part, for destroying their own environment. During the 1992/93 drought in Zimbabwe, it was difficult to distinguish the wasteland in parks caused by elephants from the wasteland outside caused by people and cattle forced to live on inhospitable land.

In short, preservationist strategies, as they are currently constituted, have:

- Made criminals of rural Africans;
- Made protected areas untenable;
- Ensured conflict around protected areas;
- Been unenforceable;
- Removed traditional controls and incentives;
- Made wildlife an open-access resource;
- Made wildlands uncompetitive;
- Encouraged crops and cattle;
- Brought marginal lands under the plough;

The value of wildlife
Progress, under these conditions, requires changing the dominant paradigm. We must not focus on taking value *away* from wildlife, but on finding ways to *increase* its value. This is the basis of the 'southern African experience.' Several studies have demonstrated that on the arid and semi-arid savannas of east and southern Africa, wildlife can out-compete domestic livestock in terms of

both net revenue and return on investment, and that in so doing it moves from being a pest to an asset. On a large ranch in southern Zimbabwe in 1992, the net revenue from wildlife was almost double that of livestock and the return on investment more than three times higher, while in Kenya a more recent study has shown that wildlife cropping is comparable with livestock rearing, while wildlife-based tourism increases net revenues by about five times. In both studies the value of livestock was similar.

Differences in the net revenue from wildlife in these two examples arise because the Zimbabwe example had no wildlife tourism other than *sport hunting* while in Kenya there was no sport hunting at all. Where landholders have been able to combine sport hunting, cropping, and photo-tourism, net revenues have been between ten and twenty times larger than from livestock. In neither of these examples was the land in question suitable for arable agriculture. It has to be noted that, where conditions allow crops to be grown, wildlife and livestock are both uncompetitive; the Kenya study has demonstrated that arable revenues are over 100 times greater than those from livestock and more than 20 times greater than from tourism.

To garner value from wildlife use is one thing, to ensure that this contributes to conservation is another altogether. However, in southern Africa it has been clearly demonstrated that, where it has been possible for private landowners and rural communities to receive economic benefits from the wildlife on their land, they have responded by investing in the wildlife 'resource' with demonstrable conservation advantages. The earliest attempts to create conservation incentives for landholders in southern Africa were based around private property, partly because of the racial history of land tenure and governance in large parts of the region, but also because it has proved much harder to construct similar mechanisms around common property.

Conservation-based community development
Programs in which wild resources directly contribute to conservation in the communally-held areas of southern Africa are

known as Community-based Natural Resource Management [CBNRM]. These programs, such as CAMPFIRE [Communal Areas Management Program for Indigenous Resources] in Zimbabwe, ADMADE [Administrative Management Design Project] in Zambia and LIFE [Living in a Finite Environment] in Namibia, are most prominent in highly traditional and poor subsistence-farming communities located near to protected areas. These are the communities of villagers who are terrorised by wild animals and who therefore directly pay the costs of Africa's national parks.

Essentially, all that CBNRM does is return the right of rural communities to manage and use wildlife for their own benefit. And by and large they are doing it well. In many programs they are making money from wild animals, particularly through trophy hunting, and only through conservation can these benefits be continued. After only a few years, some of the trends resulting from the old practices have been reversed. The depredations of wild animals continue, but are more stoically borne. There is less unregulated hunting and more land is being allocated to wildlife, even in crowded communal areas. Protected areas are viewed more favourably, as a reservoir of economic resources rather than a haven for a dangerous nuisance.

Amongst the obvious benefits of CBNRM are often supplies of meat. However, the biggest boon to communities has been the cash brought in by tourists. In Namibia this is largely from photo-tourism. By contrast, in Zimbabwe, more than ninety percent of these earnings come from tourists who wish to hunt animals. Elephant hunting alone has contributed a massive 64 percent of annual income—making this species the mainstay of the CAMPFIRE program. All the more reason for communities to carefully manage their elephant resources.

To give an idea of the benefits being realised by villagers, and the way in which they are managing these, it is helpful to examine the case of Masoka in northern Zimbabwe. From 1990 until 1994 the total revenue from CAMPFIRE, which was returned to the people of Masoka, increased by eight times from Z$78,170 to Z$639,290.

In 1994, every Masoka household earned Z$3000 from wildlife revenues. Each household allocated approximately 50 percent of the money received to community development projects, invested about 20 percent in further resource management, and kept roughly $1000 in cash. In a community in which—at that time—the average annual household income was below $300, wildlife was a very big earner indeed. One can, perhaps, guess that the attitude of the people of Masoka towards wildlife changed for the better.

The people of Masoka demonstrated that peasant farmers can make rational choices about resource management and the way that income from wildlife resources are best deployed for community benefit. In that latter regard, the way that the community managed its wildlife revenue year by year is instructive. In 1991, following severe drought and almost total crop failure, the allocation of funds to household dividends and drought relief jumped to almost 80 percent. By contrast, 1990, 1993 and 1994 revenues were used primarily for community projects and resource management. The community was shrewdly using its wildlife revenues flexibly, in good years for community development and in bad years to ensure food security.

It would be nice at this point to claim that all is rosy in these community programs in Africa. But of course that is not the case. There is nothing simple about CBNRM, especially in a politically volatile environment such as that occurring in today's Zimbabwe. Even if successful, schemes in which the value of 'wild' species is used as a conservation tool will bring their own, predictable, challenges.

Perhaps the best that can be said about CBNRM is that it is an honest attempt to do the right thing under conditions where the alternatives show even less promise. At the end of the day, CBNRM does not have to be perfect, it only has to be better than the alternative—which isn't too difficult.

The Impact of CITES

It is at this point that CITES becomes relevant to the conservation efforts of southern Africa. Whether on private or community property, the common features of programs of sustainable use are, first of all, access to the wildlife resource(s), and then, access to markets. Access to resources is, by and large, an internal policy matter—access to markets most definitely is not.

Trade in wildlife is controlled by one of the best known MEAs (multilateral environmental agreements), namely CITES (the *Convention on International Trade in Endangered Species*). This convention determines the terms of trade for wildlife products; it essentially decides what can be traded and with whom and under what conditions and—by extension—at what price. As a result, it has an enormous impact on efforts to provide the necessary incentives to halt habitat destruction by allowing wild ecosystems to be financially competitive. Small wonder then that CITES is taken very seriously by southern African countries.

Live animals in their natural habitat do, of course, have value, which can be realised through, e.g., photo-tourism. In addition, CITES places no direct impediment on the domestic use of wildlife for meat and even the marketing of derivatives and products. These activities take place in southern Africa and are important contributors to conservation, but the real value—the big money—lies in the export of durable wildlife products such as hunting trophies. When we have these export possibilities, wildlife can easily out-compete domestic stock in the marginal semi-arid rangelands of southern Africa.

Conclusion

From the southern African perspective, we can assemble the following summary concerning conservation:

• The greatest erosion of productivity and biodiversity is due to human agricultural activities, most notably the clearing of wild habitats to convert land to conventional agricultural which, due to systems of perverse incentives, offer people greater and more immediate benefits.

- The use of wild species is widespread, enormous and essential to the survival of millions of people. It cannot be stopped.

- The success of conventional conservation, in which the legal value of wild species is removed, has proved to be poor.

- Paradoxically, conservation has been successfully achieved by ensuring that people can use the very resources we wish to see conserved.

- The exploitation of wild resources may be one of the few effective mechanisms to combat the erosion of wild habitats that results from perverse incentives.

In conclusion, therefore, if viewed in the broader context of land use, it is clear that the exploitation of wild species can be either a problem or a solution, depending on a range of factors. In some cases it has been successfully harnessed to produce effective conservation.

Economic and Cultural Aspects of Polar Bear Sport Hunting in Nunavut, Canada

George W. Wenzel and Martha Dowsley
Department of Geography
McGill University, Montreal

Introduction

No animal has as large a symbolic place in Canadian Inuit culture as the polar bear (*nanuq,* in the Inuit language). Along with their cultural symbolism, polar bears have been, and continue to be, an important component of the Inuit subsistence system; today this species has assumed, through the activity of outfitted sport hunting, an economic role in the lives of Inuit that may be larger than at any time in the past. The focus of this paper is on the unique subsistence contribution of polar bears to small Nunavut communities, with some attention given to conflicts arising in allocating community polar bear quotas to sport hunters.

Polar bear sport hunting developed slowly during the 1970s in a few areas of the NWT, and, even in the early 1980s, typically accounted for only a few animals in each region. But by the mid-1980s, sport hunting underwent significant growth, increasing both as a percentage of community polar bear quotas and in overall economic terms. The collapse of the sealskin sector of the subsistence economy, coupled with the interruption of narwhal ivory sales (both due to animal protection campaigns) severely reduced hunters' incomes. As a deliberate effort to alleviate the resulting social impact, the government identified tourism, which included sport hunting, as one mechanism for enhancing community economic development.

The Nunavut Sport Hunt

The present situation in Nunavut is that polar bear sport hunting offers the opportunity for individual Inuit and their communities to obtain considerably larger sums of scarce money than is possible through more traditional means (e.g., the sale of furs) or 'green'

37

(non-consumptive) ecotourism. As a business, the sport hunt is a fairly recent development; however, for those Inuit whose whole occupation is harvesting, income obtained through guiding non-resident sport hunters is critical to their overall subsistence involvement. The most obvious aspect of the sport hunt's economic importance to Inuit outfitters, guides and hunt-assistants is for the purchase and maintenance of hunting equipment without requiring diversion of valuable time to petty wage-earning opportunities. Moreover, these monies are also important to meet the general costs that are now part of daily life.

Here we examine four Nunavut communities that recently and/or currently host polar bear sport hunting: Clyde River, Resolute, Taloyoak, and Qikiqtarjuak.

Clyde River, with an estimated population of 870, is located on the east coast of Baffin Island and about 750 km north-northwest of Iqaluit. The 2000-2001 polar bear quota in Clyde River was 21 (14 males/7 females). At present, Clyde River has three outfitters, eight licensed guides (including two of the outfitters) and a number of other men who work as guides or assistants. The local Hunters' and Trappers' Organization (HTO) decides the number of polar bear tags to be allocated to the sport hunt from the overall community bear quota. In 2000-2001 for example, ten of the 21 available tags were allocated to the three outfitters.

Resolute, with a population of 165 Inuit, is a High Arctic community having one of the largest community polar bear quotas (35 bears: 24 male/11 female) in Nunavut; the community has five guides and one local outfitter. The HTO executive committee allocates polar bear tags through a lottery system open to all HTO members. It also decides how many of the tags from the overall allocation may be sold by the tag holders to the single local outfitter for sport hunt use. The outfitter then purchases the lottery-distributed tags from individual tag holders willing to sell tags.

Taloyoak, with a population of ca. 900 Inuit, is located on the west side of Boothia Isthmus. The recent polar bear quota of 19 animals

(13 males/6 females) is a significant reduction from the community's previous official allocation of 27 bears, a reduction caused by the U.S. Fish and Wildlife Service-imposed MMPA (*Marine Mammal Protection Act)* ban on importing polar bear trophies from the McClintock Channel area into the U.S. The HTO, which serves as the sole outfitter in the community, decides how many polar bear tags to allocate to sport hunting.

Qikiqtarjuak, with a population of ca. 520 Inuit, is located on the east coast of Baffin Island, south of Clyde River. The polar bear quota in 2003-2004 was 21 animals (14 males/7 females), out of which 10 tags were allocated to the sport hunt, which in this community is also organized and outfitted by the HTO. There are four local guides; their assistants are selected by the HTO from a sign-up list. The number of tags for the sport hunt is decided by the HTO, which uses the profit from the sport hunt to purchase hunting equipment (most notably a large community boat in the 1990s) and to provide country food to the community's elders and single mothers.

Economic Considerations

In general, the economic reality of Nunavut's smaller communities is that Inuit live in a mixed or dual economy where traditional (e.g., local foods, equipment) and non-traditional (e.g., money, imported equipment) resources co-exist. Money is now essential because food capture requires purchasing, maintaining and operating an expensive set of tools (including snowmobiles, boats and motors, and rifles).

The polar bear sport hunt injects large sums of money into participating Nunavut communities, and importantly it places a considerable portion of this new money directly into the hands of those Inuit who are the most intensive harvesters.

Table 1 summarizes some of the salient elements of the sport hunt and its products within these four communities.

Table 1: Summary Of Polar Bear Sport Hunt Attributes[1]

GENERAL ATTRIBUTES	CLYDE RIVER	QIKIQTARJUAK	TALOYOAK	RESOLUTE
A) Annual Polar Bear Quota	21	21	20	35
B) Annual Sport Hunts	10	10	10	20
C) Local Outfitters	3 (private)	1 (community)	1 (community)	1 (private)
D) Wholesale Hunt Price[2]	$30,000	$30,000	$29,000	$34,500
E) Local Outfitter Price[3]	$18,400	$19,000	$13,000	$19,000
LOCAL DISTRIBUTION				
F) No.of Guides/Helpers	10/10	4/6	5/9	5/9
G) Guides' Wages	$51,000	$70,000	$47,300	$180,000
H) Helpers' Wages	$41,000	$45,000	$38,200	$100,000
I) Gratuities (average)	$1,800	$1,100	$1,500	$2,300
J) Equipment Capitalization[4]	$42,000	$8,000	Unknown	$ 34,000
K) Polar Bear Meat (kg)	2,000	2,000	1,700	6,400
L) PB Meat $ Value[5]	$17,000	$17,000	$10,000	$54,400

[1] Not factored in are fees to polar bear tag holders, additional charter or scheduled airline fares, local purchases of arts and handicrafts, and the cost of hunt consumables (e.g., food).
[2] Total fee paid to southern broker by the individual hunter for his/her hunt (CDN$).
[3] Contract fee between southern-based wholesaler and local outfitters.
[4] These data refer to equipment purchased with sport hunt wages and are only partial.
[5] Based on $8.50 per kg for imported meat (averaged across the communities).
[6] As polar bear meat is generally used for dog fodder at Taloyoak, the value imputed to the meat entering the community is based on the price of imported dry dog food.

As Table 2 indicates, the returns to individuals and communities that participate in the sport polar bear hunt are by no means small. In gross terms, a guide from Clyde River can potentially receive up to $7,250 from a single hunt and it is not uncommon for a man to guide twice (occasionally three times) in a season which generally lasts no more than two months.

In Resolute, each guide works four hunts, and in Taloyoak usually two. In addition, the general population of sport hunt communities receives polar bear meat; in Clyde River, for example, the sport hunts provide the community with approximately 2,000 kg of fresh meat. Furthermore, while it is the case that the polar bear hunt itself demands a considerable investment of time away from the community, even a full hunt (most hunts have a maximum length of ten days) sees a guide earn an hourly wage of roughly $30.

Table 2: Sport Hunt Benefits[1]

Community	Workers [2]	Person Days	Wages	Cash Tips	Equipment[3]	Country Food[4]
Clyde River	10	178	$92,000	$16,845	$6,000	$14,000 (10)
Qikiqtarjuak	10	200	$115,000	$11,000	$8,000	$14,000 (10)
Resolute	12	356	$280,000	$33,690	$12,000	$28,000 (20)
Taloyoak	10	162	$85,500	$9,000	???	$10,000 (10)

[1] These data relate to the Spring 2000 hunt season.
[2] Includes guides and hunt assistants (data on person days, wages and cash and in-kind gratuities include both categories of "workers").
[3] Estimate of the value of received items.
[4] Estimated replacement cost of imported meat purchased at $10.00 per kg.

Management-Related Conflicts

Conflicts around the sport hunt almost invariably involve issues relating to the way the basic management of polar bears is conducted. For example, Taloyoak, which only undertook polar bear sport hunting in the mid-1990s, had its hunt shut down after the 2000 season because a statistical analysis of the number of marked animals in the catch suggested that far fewer bears were present than had been assumed when the quota was established. On the basis of this analysis, the estimate for the McClintock Channel population was revised downward from 850-900 to no more than 250 animals. This conclusion prompted the U.S. Fish and Wildlife Service to ban the importation of McClintock Channel polar bear hides into the United States. As a result, American hunters, who until 2000 had formed the entire sport-hunter clientele at Taloyoak, ceased to book hunts in the area, representing a loss of some $95,000 in guide and hunt assistant wages in Taloyoak.

The chief point of conflict in this particular case is that the original analysis that ultimately resulted in the import ban was not discussed with the affected local communities before these regulatory decisions were taken. Especially irksome to the Inuit, is that no effort was made to incorporate or even elicit their knowledge and observations about trends in the McClintock Channel bear population at any point in the analysis or in the decision process.

Qikiqtarjuak, like Taloyoak and Clyde River, also exploits a regional bear population from which hides have been embargoed by the United States, and thus is unable to attract clients from that country. Where the sport hunt situation differs for Qikiqtarjuak (and for Clyde River) relative to that of Taloyoak, is that the U.S. problem is not caused by a belief that there are too few bears in the Baffin Bay population, as is the case for the McClintock Channel population, but rather from the lack of a polar bear management plan by the Greenland's Home Rule government (which similarly is cause for invoking MMPA sanctions). However, Qikiqtarjuak and Clyde River, while unable to attract American hunters, are able to draw sportsmen from Europe, Japan and South America and so are far less economically disadvantaged by the absence of U.S. hunters.

Culture-Based Conflicts

Another serious conflict relates to views about the propriety of polar bear sport hunting itself. In this case, some Clyde River Inuit believe that sport hunting, and indeed efforts at conservation-management, are antithetical to maintaining an appropriate ethical relationship between people and polar bears. The concern here is the implied presumption that people can directly influence animal behavior, in this case by taking fewer animals than (according to Inuit belief) choose to make themselves available to worthy hunters. Secondarily, it was felt that the establishment of a quota—and indeed even a population census—would cause polar bears to think that hunters were bragging about their own prowess and were consequently being disrespectful to *nanuq*. Such inappropriate human behavior would cause the animals to move to areas where humans would be respectful.

Despite these expressions of dissatisfaction, over the next decade Clyde River hunters adhered, with only the occasional exception, to the polar bear regulations. However, even with this high degree of compliance, the polar bear quota was reduced from 45 to 21 bears in the 1980s, an action interpreted in Clyde River as tacit proof of the inappropriateness of the management regime. Recently, intense competition for clients by the several local outfitters has increasingly come to be seen by community members as also potentially offensive to polar bears. Because of this possibility, the HTO membership decided that in 2003 the sport allocation would be reduced to five animals and that the HTO would be the sole outfitter.

Conclusions

At present, Inuit receive barely one-half (<$1.5 million) of the monies actually paid (approx. $2.9 million) by sport hunters to Nunavut. Nevertheless, these not insignificant revenues mostly go directly into the hands of Inuit who choose to spend much time hunting and bringing local food into the community. So sport hunting has social importance beyond its strictly economic benefit.

Nunavut Inuit, although free to assign 100 percent of their community bear quota should they wish, in fact allocate barely 25 percent of the polar bear quota in any year to sport hunting. This obvious non-maximizing approach toward the one 'commodity' able to generate significant monetary income from the application of traditional Inuit skills, suggests that the cultural value Inuit place on *nanuq* is decidedly more important to them than the economic return that polar bears might provide.

Another point that should be emphasized, is that even as highly (and wisely) managed as polar bear are in Nunavut, conflicts arise with disconcerting frequency. Related to this, while the most visible and strident of these disagreements are between Inuit and management agencies, there is also friction among Inuit about contemporary polar bear use. These range from issues of equitable access to polar bears at the local level, to deeply felt cultural matters concerning the propriety of such activities.

That disagreement occurs between Inuit and non-Inuit over polar bear, despite inordinate flexibility in the regulatory system, should not be surprising. First, Inuit neither had initial input, nor have significant input today, into the international polar bear agreement which underlies current polar bear management decisions. Furthermore, that the traditional knowledge of those with by far the longest experience with polar bear is rarely incorporated in any effectively meaningful way into the regulatory system or its science, continues to provoke continuing disagreement.

Interestingly, if the matter of best, if not wise, use were strictly the province of non-Inuit wildlife managers and economic planners, Nunavut Inuit might be encouraged to take full economic advantage of their quotas. In such a case, better use would mean allocating more, if not all, of an annual quota to the sport hunt, since even at the current overall price per hunt (approximately Can$35,000), such a practice would inject as much as $14 million into Nunavut's

44

cash-poor communities. It is thus no small irony that Inuit culture provides an effective brake on even wider economic exploitation of polar bear.

The Barren-Ground Caribou Sports Hunt in the North Slave Region, Northwest Territories, Canada

H. Dean Cluff and Ernie Campbell
Resources, Wildlife and Economic Development
Government of the Northwest Territories, Yellowknife

Introduction

The commercial outfitting industry in the Northwest Territories (NWT) began in 1959 when hunts for bison were offered. Hunts expanded to the Mackenzie Mountains in 1965 when big-game outfitters were permitted to operate there. Outfitted hunts for polar bear in the NWT (which included Nunavut at the time) followed in 1969/70. The following year, several Inuvialuit communities, through their Hunters' and Trappers' Committees (HTC), offered similar hunts for polar bear. In 1979, the HTC outfitters expanded their hunts by including muskox.

Subsequent changes to NWT wildlife legislation in 1982 allowed outfitted hunts for barren-ground caribou. At that time, five barren-ground caribou outfitters were licensed in the North Slave Region. Provision was also made for community-based outfitting through their respective Hunters' and Trappers' Association (HTA). The profile of the hunt was raised in 1984 when the Boone and Crocket Club created a separate trophy listing for 'Central Canadian Barren-ground Caribou.' In 1987, an additional two outfitting licenses became available but were not issued until 1993.

Currently, only residents living in the Northwest Territories for at least two continuous years do not require the services of an outfitter to hunt big game. Other Canadian residents or landed immigrants ('non-residents' [NR]) and non-Canadians ('non-resident aliens' [NRA]) require an outfitter to hunt big game, but not small game, in the NWT. For outfitters operating in the North Slave Region of the NWT, big game available for sports hunts includes barren-ground caribou, wolf, wolverine, and black bear. Although present in the area, there is no open season for barren-ground grizzly bears in the NWT portion of their range.

Economic Benefits of the Barren-Ground Caribou Outfitting Industry

Economics of barren-ground caribou outfitting in the Northwest Territories has grown significantly since its inception in the early 1980s, and much of these benefits have accrued to the NWT. In 1999, the industry grossed over $3 Million among the 10 outfitters (HTA and non-HTA). Non-resident hunters further spent upwards of $1 Million on non-outfitter purchases within the NWT.

The number of jobs estimated to have resulted from the barren-ground caribou outfitting industry in 1999 was 179 direct seasonal jobs with another 63 direct seasonal jobs from non-outfitter related expenditures by hunters. Outfitted hunters at camps harvested about 41,500 kg of caribou meat, having an estimated replacement value of $395,000. Although about 10% of the meat is consumed while at camp, amounts vary among outfitters. Caribou meat is also given to guides and other outfitter staff for personal consumption at home.

License revenues

Most non-resident hunters represent 'new' money into the territory. On average, about 14 percent of non-resident hunters hunting barren-ground caribou in Unit R (North Slave Region, see below) are from within Canada. Of those non-resident hunters from outside Canada (NRA hunters), about three-quarters are from the USA. Since 1997, an average of about $139,000/year has been received from license fees, although over $180,000 was collected in 2002. Similarly, trophy fees collected since 1997 have averaged about $174,000 and peaked in 1999 at over $250,000.

Hunt Management

The NWT sets wildlife harvesting regulations based on Wildlife Management Units (WMU). Names and boundaries of WMUs have been revised over time and now reflect completed and pending land claims by Aboriginal groups. Barren-ground caribou outfitters in

North Slave Region operate within WMU R, which reflects current boundaries in the *Tli Cho (Dogrib) Final Land Claim Agreement*. Unlike outfitting areas in the Gwich'in (WMU G), Sahtu region (WMU S), and the Deh Cho region (WMU D), outfitting areas in Unit R are not legally defined. Consequently, there is no legal provision to guarantee one outfitters' exclusive use of a given area within Unit R. However, in practice, the existing outfitters are spread out geographically within the WMU largely as a result of a 'gentleman's agreement.'

Outfitter licenses are issued depending on whether a Hunters' and Trappers' Association (HTA), or a company operating on its behalf, is the operator of the business. An HTA outfitting license provides authorization to hunt grizzly bear, black bear, polar bear, barren-ground caribou, muskox, wolf, wolverine, and wood bison in the area that the HTA serves. A non-HTA outfitting license can be issued to any person to hunt barren-ground caribou, black bear, wolf, and wolverine in WMUs R, S, and U. A maximum of 10 HTA outfitter licenses may be issued for WMUs R, S and U, while a maximum of seven non-HTA outfitter licenses may be issued for these three units.

Seasons, tag allocations, and fees
The hunting season opens for barren-ground caribou on 15 August and closes 30 November, although most hunting activity has been completed by late September. Contributing factors to this short season is the migration of the caribou south and the reliance of most of these camps on floatplane access.

The number of tags available for outfitted caribou hunts began with 32 in 1992. Currently, distribution of tags is based on whether outfitters are classified as either HTA or non-HTA. For non-HTA outfitters, 1260 tags are available for caribou. Therefore, 180 tags are available for each outfitter, assuming the full complement of seven non-HTA outfitters for Unit R. However, if there are fewer than seven non-HTA outfitters operating or not all outfitters can use their individual allotment of 180 tags, then tags may be re-assigned for a given year upon application by one of the outfitters.

The maximum number of tags available to any non-HTA outfitter is 310.

The maximum number of caribou tags available to HTA outfitters is 132 each. Currently, there are three HTA outfitters; therefore 396 tags are available for this group. Application for additional tags is not routinely considered because these caribou tags have been transferred from the commercial hunt quota of 1260 tags. If an HTA wants to change the number of tags available for outfitting, then a request must be made to the Minister to reallocate tags from the commercial meat quota (*Sale of Wildlife Regulations*) to the outfitting quota (*Big Game Hunting Regulations*). Caribou tags issued to an HTA outfitter, or a company operating on its behalf, must use the tags for hunts by NR and NRA hunting license holders.

Meat from outfitted hunts

Wastage of big game meat suitable for human consumption is an offence under the *NWT Wildlife Act*. Consequently, a meat distribution form is provided to all hunters, outfitters and guides to complete, detailing the distribution and disposal of meat from each caribou killed. Completion of this form is required as a condition of a Big Game Outfitting License. Hunters leaving the NWT with any parts of their caribou require an export permit and are subject to trophy fees.

Bathurst caribou herd management plan

In April 2000, a *Bathurst Barren Ground Caribou Management Planning Agreement* was signed by the federal and territorial governments, and Aboriginal groups. A Bathurst Caribou Management Committee has since prepared a 10-year management plan for the Bathurst caribou herd and its habitat. Consultation and partnership with Aboriginal groups is critical for effective management because of the likelihood that some management actions could influence Aboriginal harvesting rights. Outfitted hunts do not enjoy this level of legal support, and therefore they did not warrant inclusion as a separate party to the *Agreement*.

The outfitted caribou hunt seldom exceeds 1150 animals, of which the hunt targets bulls only. In fact, in only 2 of the last 8 years has the kill in Unit R by non-resident hunters exceeded 1000 caribou; the hunt has not yet maximized its full tag allocation. Of 1656 tags potentially available, the number of tags sold peaked in 2002 at 1425 tags held by 814 hunters. The previous year recorded a high of 860 hunters participating in the hunt, but has declined since. The 2004 outfitted caribou hunt recorded 1163 tags sold and 912 caribou killed by 648 hunters.

The harvest of wolf and wolverine is opportunistic and significantly more tags have been sold than animals killed. The number of wolves and wolverines harvested has increased slightly in recent years and might reflect a greater effort for these carnivore species, or a change in hunting strategies, or both.

Using the Hunt to Improve Wildlife Monitoring of the Area

The outfitting industry understands the need for monitoring programs, research and reporting. Consequently, outfitters have participated in several initiatives that benefit management of the resource and include:

- Collection of infected or diseased tissue samples.
- Collecting DNA samples from wolves and wolverine.
- Complete carcass collection for wolverine.
- Reporting grizzly bear sightings.

Issues Facing the Industry

Several issues are facing the barren-ground outfitting industry relating to both their specific operations and indirect impacts. These include:

- Tracking caribou meat from hunts.
- Allocation of tags for outfitters with declining numbers of caribou.
- Defined hunting areas for each outfitter.
- Grizzly bears killed in defense of life and property.

- Potential impacts associated with the settlement of Aboriginal land claims.
- Cumulative effects of increased human activity and economic development taking place in the North.

Conclusions

The barren-ground caribou outfitting in the North Slave Region is a successful industry and is well managed. Challenges remain however, but the government continues to work with outfitters to address their needs while ensuring the hunt remains sustainable. Consequently, the industry maintains a bright future. Wildlife monitoring of caribou and other wildlife can be enhanced with the participation of outfitters.

Co-Management and Conservation Hunting in the Western Canadian Arctic

Frank Pokiak
Chair, Inuvialuit Game Council
Inuvik, Northwest Territories

Introduction

Aboriginal land claims between the Inuvialuit residents of the Western Canadian Arctic and the Government of Canada were completed and came into effect through passage of the *Western Arctic (Inuvialuit) Claims Settlement Act* in the Canadian Parliament in 1984. The resulting *Inuvialuit Final Agreement (IFA)* takes precedence over all other legislation in the event of any inconsistency.

The goals of the IFA are to:

- preserve Inuvialuit cultural identity and values within a changing northern society;
- enable Inuvialuit to be equal and meaningful participants in the northern and national economy and society;
- protect and preserve arctic wildlife, environment and biological activity.

In this paper, I wish to discuss this third goal in further detail.

Inuvialuit Settlement Region (ISR)

The ISR is the Inuvialuit land claim settlement area, an area extending over one million square kilometers and comprising Inuvialuit Private Land, Crown Land, and the Eastern Beaufort Sea. Within this area are the Inuvialuit communities of Aklavik, Inuvik, Paulatuk and Tuktoyaktuk (all on the mainland) Holman (on western Victoria Island) and Sachs Harbour (on southwest Banks Island).

Inuvialuit Game Council (IGC)

The IGC was established under the terms of the IFA. The IGC consists of representatives of the Hunters' and Trappers' Committees (HTCs) from each of the six Inuvialuit communities. Each HTC appoints a Director and an Alternate to sit on the IGC. The Chair of the IGC is elected by the HTC Boards.

The responsibilities of the IGC include:

- representing the collective Inuvialuit interest in wildlife;
- appointing Inuvialuit to sit on co-management boards and other bodies;
- advising the government on wildlife issues;
- assigning community hunting and trapping areas;
- allocating wildlife quotas among the communities.

Hunters and Trappers Committees (HTCs)

Some of the duties of the HTCs include:

- advising the IGC on wildlife issues;
- sub-allocating wildlife quotas to HTC members;
- establishing community wildlife by-laws;
- assisting in providing harvest data to the co-management bodies.

Co-management Bodies

There are five co-management bodies established under the IFA. These are the:

- Wildlife Management Advisory Council (Northwest Territories);
- Wildlife Management Advisory Council (North Slope);
- Fisheries Joint Management Committee;
- Environmental Impact Screening Committee;
- Environmental Impact Review Board.

One half of the members of each co-management board, council or committee are Inuvialuit, and half are government representatives.

The Chair of each board, council or committee is jointly agreed upon by both parties.

The Wildlife Management Advisory Council for the NWT (WMAC-NWT) is responsible for the co-management of game species for the NWT portion of the ISR. WMAC-North Slope is responsible for co-management of game species in Inuvialuit lands bordering the Beaufort Sea west of the Mackenzie Delta.

Wildlife Management Advisory Council for the Northwest Territories
The duties of WMAC-NWT include the following:

- advising government on wildlife matters in the Western Arctic Region;
- advising and providing information to Inuvialuit boards and co-management bodies;
- determining and recommending quotas for Inuvialuit harvesting.

Two examples are provided here to illustrate the success of the co-management process. These are the *International Polar Bear Management Agreement*, and the establishment of polar bear and grizzly bear quotas in the ISR.

International Polar Bear Management Agreement
This international agreement, reached between the Inuvialuit of Canada and the Iñupiat of Alaska, is recognized as one of the first international wildlife management agreements concluded between two aboriginal bodies. The agreement was initially signed in 1988 and was updated in 2000. A report titled *The Polar Bear Management Agreement for the Southern Beaufort Sea: An Evaluation of the First Ten Years of a Unique Conservation Agreement* has been published (in *Arctic* 55(4):362-372, December 2002).

Representatives from Alaska and Canada meet annually to share research information, including traditional knowledge, relating to the South Beaufort Sea polar bear population. Recent mark and recapture work is showing that the population is healthy, an observation also being made by Inuvialuit and Iñupiat hunters.

As a consequence of successful co-management arrangements, Inuvialuit are able to offer sport hunts for the South Beaufort Sea polar bear population (hunted by the four Inuvialuit communities situated on the mainland) and the North Beaufort Sea and Viscount Melville populations to the northeast (hunted from Inuvialuit communities on Banks and Victoria islands).

Sport hunting over the years has become an important source of income for some Inuvialuit hunters who have chosen to become outfitters or guides. The IGC has worked to insure that the subsistence needs of communities are met before tags are allocated to sport hunters. To this end, the IGC passed a resolution which allows no more than 50 percent of polar bear tags to be used for sport hunts. This has created a balance between the subsistence needs of Inuvialuit and the additional economic benefits that sport hunters bring to Inuvialuit communities.

Grizzly Bear Quotas in the ISR

When the IFA was signed in 1984, it gave the Inuvialuit exclusive hunting rights to several species in the ISR; one of these species was the grizzly bear. At the time the IFA was signed, there were no grizzly bear quotas in place. Within a short time following the IFA, Inuvialuit hunters in Tuktoyaktuk realized that due to the unsustainable level of hunting, grizzly bears needed to be subject to conservation action. As a consequence, and utilizing the co-management process, a grizzly bear quota was established by the Inuvialuit and the NWT Territorial Government. Shortly after this action was taken, other Inuvialuit communities also established grizzly bear quotas.

Since these early post-IFA years, the Inuvialuit have worked closely with government to ensure that hunting levels remain at sustainable levels. This co-operation has been very successful. This year (2004), based on scientific research and traditional knowledge, the quota for the eastern ISR region was increased from 22 to 31 grizzly bears, a quota shared by three communities. As with polar bears, the IGC allows no more than 50 percent of grizzly bear tags to be allocated to the sport hunt, thus meeting the subsistence needs of the communities while bringing additional needed economic benefits into the region.

Conclusions

The overall approach to polar bear and grizzly bear management has created and sustained a situation where both species are recognized as highly valued resources. As a result of this high value placed on bears, there are a minimal number of problem bears taken each year (every problem bear taken results in a loss of a tag from the community quota, thus providing a strong disincentive for needlessly shooting potential problem animals).

The co-management process has certainly worked well for the Inuvialuit. At times there are disagreements between government and the Inuvialuit on some issues, but through discussion, mutually agreeable conclusions are reached. As a result, grizzly and polar bears are being successfully managed and we continue to work to ensure that healthy wildlife populations exist within the Inuvialuit region of the Western Canadian Arctic.

Multilateral Environmental Agreements and the Future of Hunting

Kai Wollscheid

CIC- International Council for Game and Wildlife Conservation
Budapest, Hungary

Introduction

Hunting is one measure for more effectively 'integrating people with wildlife.' However, in a rapidly urbanizing world, trophy hunting has something of a bad image with the public at large, being variously associated with overexploitation, species extinction, and taking resources away from indigenous peoples.

However, Klaus Topfer, Executive Director of the UN Environment Program (UNEP), has observed:

> *There will be those who view hunting, particularly in rich and developed countries, as outdated and unnecessary··· However, carefully managed and controlled hunting has its role to play in delivering conservation and enriching our links with the natural world.*

Such hunting activities are recognized as providing important economic and conservation benefits. Thus, in 2004, the UNEP World Conservation Monitoring Centre stated:

> *The increasing number of hunting reserves in Africa and elsewhere are often carefully managed to maintain the game and predator animals they need for commercial hunting, and the high value of these animals often ensures effective anti-poaching operations.*

On a regional level, the Parliamentary Assembly of the Council of Europe, uniting 46 member states with 800 million Europeans, has noted:

> *Hunting and hunting-tourism must play their proper role as stimulus to sustainable economic and natural development.*

MEAs Relevant for Hunting

There are a number of international and regional Multilateral Environmental Agreements (MEAs) that may be briefly considered, including the *Convention on Biological Diversity* (CBD), the *Convention on Migratory Species* (CMS), the *Convention on International Trade in Endangered Species* (CITES), and the *African Convention on the Conservation of Nature and Natural Resources.* In addition, there are other international organizations, including the UN Food & Agriculture Organization (FAO) and the UN Educational and Scientific Organization (UNESCO) and the International Union for the Conservation of Nature (IUCN), that are of relevance for hunting in a wider perspective.

The Convention on Biological Diversity (CBD)

The CBD has three main goals: the conservation of biological diversity, the sustainable use of its component species, and the fair and equitable sharing of the benefits derived from the use of these resources. In this respect, the *Convention* offers a comprehensive global strategy for a wider range of 'thematic programs,' such as mountain or forest biodiversity, as well as 'cross-cutting' issues like sustainable use or tourism.

Important recent international tools under the CBD include the *Addis Ababa Principles and Guidelines for the Sustainable Use of Biodiversity* (AAPG) concerned with ensuring that uses of renewable living resources are sustainable. Rather than urging governments to adopt a number of (inflexible) legal prescriptions, the AAPG provide a framework for advising governments, resource managers, indigenous and local communities, the private sector and other stakeholders on the measures and principles than can encourage sustainable use. The AAPG recognize and encourage the users and managers to pragmatically adapt these principles and guidelines so as to best fit local circumstances, while explicitly recognizing that (1) wildlife use is a crucial sector in many communities' circumstances, and (2) the importance of hunting to achieving biodiversity conservation.

Indeed, several of the programs and issues under the *Convention* include hunting as a valuable tool for wildlife conservation, as e.g., the program of work on mountain biodiversity, which seeks to

> *promote sustainable land-use practices··· including those of indigenous and local communities and community-based management systems, for the conservation and sustainable use (including pastoralism, hunting and fishing) of wild flora and fauna···*

In another of its programs (Biodiversity and Tourism Development), CBD notes that in some respects hunting tourism, if well regulated, may be comparable to eco-tourism. In relation to the need for regulation, CBD suggests the need to develop standards, and possibly certification schemes, within a regionally-appropriate approach to the issue.

The Convention on Migratory Species (CMS)
With regard to regionally-appropriate measures, this global convention also encourages range states to conclude regional agreements (as well as, when appropriate, global agreements). An example of such a regional approach is that taken by four Central Asian range states (Kazakhstan, Tajikistan, Turkmenistan and Uzbekistan) in respect to the Bukhara deer, a species threatened by, e.g., habitat destruction and illegal hunting. The range states, working with WWF and CIC, have cooperated on programs of habitat conservation, reintroduction of deer, establishing protected areas, and various anti-poaching initiatives. Some of the successes of these cooperative programs include stabilized and increasing deer populations in two of the range states, a significant increase in

the overall Bukhara deer population, and the recognition by many people in the region that this species is a valued national treasure having recognized global importance.

The Convention of International Trade in Endangered Species (CITES)

Although CITES focuses its actions on identifying species considered to be at various degrees of endangerment and then limiting or banning trade in these species or their products, it increasingly recognizes the value of sustainable use (including hunting) as an acceptable wildlife conservation measure. This has been the case with, e.g., the black rhinoceros, elephants, leopards, certain crocodiles, and markhor.

The African Convention on the Conservation of Nature and Natural Resources

This is a regional wildlife conservation convention (a revision of the so-called *Algiers Convention* that dates back to 1968) adopted in 2003 by 28 nations. It is the most modern and comprehensive MEA, and it reflects processes advocated by CBD and other appropriate international agreements (including the *African Charter on Human and Peoples' Rights*). Accordingly, it has great potential for conservation and sustainable use of wildlife by providing practical guidelines for implementation while urging signatories to enhance legislation relating to all forms of wildlife use. Its progressive nature makes it an excellent example for other regional wildlife management treaties to follow.

FAO Forest Resource Assessment (FRA) 2000

The FRA, in addition to assessing the importance of forests as sources of timber and wood products, also recognizes that non-wood forest products are major sources of food and income, noting:

> *Hunting game meat and animal trophies provide significant income to both private forest owners and public land management agencies.*

Whilst recognizing the serious lack of data available from many countries, the FRA 2000 report provides estimates for the value of game meat hunted in some European countries: US$76.1 Million in Sweden, US$66.5 Million in Norway (1994-96), and US$64.0 Million in Finland (1996). These figures likely do not include the subsistence use of these wildlife resources by local people, as collecting such information is technically difficult and very expensive. Nevertheless, the data reported above very likely provides a minimal estimate of the value of game meat harvested in these countries.

It becomes obvious that the economic value of the wildgame harvest through hunting needs to be demonstrated through sound statistical reporting. Hence hunting organizations, as well as governmental authorities responsible for wildlife management, should engage more in collecting and presenting relevant data in recognition of mechanisms provided for by such organizations as FAO.

Some Reactionary Hold-outs

However, despite these promising newer MEA initiatives in some international fora, the recognition that wildlife possesses economic value that can support biodiversity conservation initiatives still receives little support. For example, during the 2003 IUCN World Parks Congress, CIC and FAO jointly expressed their concern that:

> ···the Congress does not recognize the importance of appropriate forms of wildlife utilization to generate revenues for conservation. Instead, overemphasis is placed on non-sustainable external funding···

The CIC-FAO commentary, being incorporated into the official Congress proceedings and forwarded by IUCN to conventions like the CBD, went on to note:

> Sustainable hunting and fishing (including trophy and subsistence hunting) and other wildlife uses contribute to biodiversity conservation by:

- *providing finance for the management of protected and non-protected natural areas;*
- *generating income and benefits for local communities and landowners;*
- *creating strong incentives to manage and conserve wildlife and its habitat;*
- *offering indigenous people economic opportunities, whilst retaining [their] rights, knowledge systems and traditions.*

In this context, it was urged that:

> *IUCN [should] identify best practices of sustainable hunting and fishing and assist in their dissemination and implementation.*

The Cultural Value of Hunting

The cultural importance of one particular way of hunting, namely falconry, has been recognized by the UN Educational and Scientific Organization (UNESCO) in its *List of Documented Heritage.* Therein, UNESCO explicitly recognizes

> *Falconry [is] common to a large number of societies. This [form of hunting] dates from the beginning of civilization and is of unusual interest because it is still practiced in numerous countries. Falconry is an important social element for an understanding of Asian and Oriental peoples··· and as a way to understand social cohesion of societies.*

Building on this existing recognition, CIC now aims to have falconry, practiced in a sustainable manner in many regions of the world, incorporated in UNESCO's *Proclamation of Masterpieces of the Oral and Intangible Heritage of Humanity.* This proclamation honours forms of popular and traditional expression (including oral histories, dance, art, rituals, customs and craftwork) and cultural spaces or sites where traditional or popular cultural activities take place on a regular or otherwise important basis. To be recognized by UNESCO as a masterpiece heritage of humanity, such cultural expressions or activities must, for example:

- *give wide evidence of their roots in the cultural traditions or history of the community;*
- *demonstrate their role as a means of affirming the cultural identity of the peoples and cultural communities concerned;*
- *demonstrate their importance as a source of inspiration and intercultural exchange as a means of bringing peoples and communities together;*
- *demonstrate their contemporary cultural and social role in the community;*
- *provide proof of excellence in the application of the skill and technical qualities displayed;*
- *affirm their value as unique testimonies of living cultural traditions;*
- *be at risk of disappearing, due either to a lack of means for safeguarding and protecting them, or [due] to processes of rapid change, urbanization or acculturation.*

All the above is also true for a number of indigenous hunting traditions. The UNESCO *Proclamation of Masterpieces of the Oral and Intangible Heritage of Humanity* is worth considering as a tool to achieve wider recognition of the value of these hunting traditions.

Conclusions

It might be useful for hunting communities to give greater attention to the supporting principles contained in a number of MEA's and to ensure their actions conform to and benefit from these agreements' implementation advice.

When seeking conservation-hunting best practices, the design and reporting provisions of some of these MEAs may be particularly helpful.

Hunting communities should recognize and utilize the political importance of linking their sustaining hunting practices to their cultural roots and persistence, and seek recognition by international agreements and frameworks as provided by the UN or relevant MEAs. The CIC is prepared to assist in these endeavours, and to offer advice to governments agencies, NGOs and the wider hunting community on suitable approaches to be taken.

Guide, Bowhunter and Polar Bear, Nunavut

Photos courtesy Fred A. Webb

Hunter and Muskox, Nunavut

Hunters and Wolf, Nunavut

Photos courtesy Fred A. Webb

Hunter, Guide and Barren-Ground Grizzly Bear, Nunavut

Hunter and Walrus, Nunavut

*Hunter and Barren-Ground
Caribou, Nunavut*

Photos courtesy Fred A. Webb

Bowhunter and Bighorn Sheep, Alberta
Photos courtesy APOS

Young Bowhunter and Moose, Alberta

Hunter and Elk, Alberta

Photos courtesy APOS

Hunter and Wood Bison, Alberta

Hunting: more than killing wildlife, Alberta

Photo courtesy APOS

Principles, Perspectives and Ethics of Conservation Hunting

Lee Foote
Department of Renewable Resources
University of Alberta

Introduction

The term 'conservation' is often used erroneously to refer to preservation. Conservation, in contrast to preservation, requires the intent to use a resource, whereas preservation refers to the intent to save the resource from being used.

Hunting is an activity that has great meaning to those who engage in it—and even to some who do not participate directly in hunting. Hunting is also a tool: it can be used to achieve important conservation goals (illustrated by several other papers in this report).

People hunt for a variety of purposes, including, e.g., to obtain food having high nutritional, cultural and/or economic value, to maintain family and cultural traditions, for personal achievement or fulfillment, for companionship, and to better appreciate nature and some exceptional animals.

The Value of Hunting

Hunting represents different values to different individuals and different sectors of society. Generally speaking, hunters, outfitters and hunting organizations, Aboriginal community members, and some landowners and business interests in hunting regions of the country appreciate many of the diverse benefits of hunting. However, among the non-hunting public, hunting may be much less appreciated. Although hunters care passionately about hunting, polls indicate that about 80 percent of the public is ambivalent toward hunting. Furthermore, most of the voting public is poorly informed about the subject.

It is probably fair to say that the general public rarely associates hunting with conservation. There is little public awareness that hunters' appreciation of wildlife has resulted in considerable financial and organizational resources being directed to the protection of wildlife habitat and recovery of many mammal and bird species. It is important to note that these recovered species are of interest not only to hunters, but also more generally, to the public at large.

Countering Public Misunderstanding

Given the existing public ambivalence or negativity toward hunters and hunting, discussion is ongoing concerning the need to effect better public relations between hunters and the public at large (and that includes the media and politicians). Establishing a hunters' Code of Ethics has been suggested as one useful public relations initiative. However, some have pointed out the difficulty, if not impossibility, of obtaining agreement on a standardized set of ethics that would satisfy hunters from different cultural communities living in a fast-changing world.

Perhaps working to develop an agreed-upon 'code of practice' would make more sense? A set of hunting 'best practices' would also serve to educate the non-hunting public, and might even encourage members of a better-informed public to, themselves, engage in hunting. Some of the principles in a Hunters' Code of Practice would require that the hunter/the hunt:

- Contributes positively to the wellbeing of local people;
- Seeks to minimize animal welfare impacts;
- Involves full utilization of each animal taken (i.e., no wanton waste);
- Ensure the hunt be biologically sustainable;
- Causes no significant genetic impacts on the species being hunted;
- Is immersed in a learning, enriching environment.

To be effective in explaining hunting to non-hunters, it is important that hunters marry hunting to widely-appreciated social values. Such values will include, e.g., conservation benefits, public safety, employment and revenue benefits for economically-disadvantaged rural communities, physical and mental health benefits (including providing families with nutritious meat, exercise and recreation, and achieving a meaningful closeness to nature).

Conclusions

Hunters are advised to be forthright and open when discussing hunting. People are often negative because of their misconceptions, but negativity and the misconceptions can be changed by talking with someone who understands hunting. For example, to many people, a hunting trophy may be thought of in very negative terms, but to hunters, a trophy may have meaning at many levels, and consequently is highly valued.

Conservation hunting may be thought of by many as a contradiction in terms. On the other hand, it provides a very useful starting point for improving others' understanding and appreciation of both hunting and conservation.

Conservation Hunting to Aid in the Persistence of Re-Introduced Wood Bison in the Yukon

Graham Van Tighem
Yukon Fish and Wildlife Management Board, Whitehorse
Thomas S. Jung
Yukon Department of Environment, Whitehorse
Michelle Oakley
Yukon Department of Environment, Haines Junction

Abstract*

Bison were once an integral part of the Beringian landscape of Yukon and Alaska, along with other ice age mammals, such as the woolly mammoth. Nobody knows when wood bison became extinct in the Yukon, but fossil horn cores have been found and dated as recently as 350 years ago. In parts of the Yukon, First Nations' peoples coexisted with the wood bison and other large herbivores (i.e., woodland caribou, moose, and wapiti) for thousands of years, but wood bison have not been a part of the landscape or culture in recent times. It appears that the connection that local peoples once enjoyed with this species had been lost.

Beginning in 1980, the Yukon Government in partnership with the Canadian Wildlife Service and the Yukon Fish and Game Association, began a project to reintroduce wood bison to the Yukon. This reintroduction project was a part of the National Wood Bison Recovery Program in Canada. The goal of the national program was to re-establish at least four viable and self-sustaining herds of free-ranging wood bison in their original range. By 1999, the Aishihik Herd in the Yukon had reached the minimum viable population size of more than 400 animals. The Yukon reintroduction project was a success: the population was established and considered viable.

However, the burgeoning and expanding wood bison population was a strong new force on the land and causing some problems.

Moreover, local people had concerns that the expanding herd would cause further problems. In essence, wood bison had become an *'overabundant endangered species.'* The cause of their apparent overabundance was not due to ecological carrying capacity, but rather, it was directly due to the social carrying capacity, or tolerance of local peoples to the presence of these new, and sometimes threatening, large animals. Despite significant preparations from the biological and technical perspective, there had been almost no First Nation involvement in the re-introduction project. This was unfortunate, given that the local peoples would now be sharing their traditional territories with the largest land mammal in North America.

There were few limiting factors on the growth of the Aishihik Herd, and predat.. n does not seem to be a regulatory factor on the herd even now. The herd grew rapidly in the absence of strong limiting factors or regulating mechanisms. To deal with the issue of overabundance and other local concerns, the Yukon Fish and Wildlife Management Board and the Yukon Territorial Government developed a management plan for bison in 1998. The management plan dealt with enhancing public support and buy-in for wood bison through a two-way information flow between Yukon communities and the Yukon Government, and increasing knowledge about wood bison in the Yukon and Canada. As set out in the 1998 plan, harvest would be the means to try to keep the Aishihik Herd within the socially acceptable population size.

However, this was not an easy decision for some, given the national status of wood bison as a Threatened Species, but the options were limited and community concerns about impacts associated with the expanding bison herd needed to be addressed. The management plan provided for the establishment of licensed harvests, largely by the two First Nations affected by the reintroduction project and other Yukon residents. What makes the Yukon wood bison harvest somewhat extraordinary is that over 90 percent of the animals taken are taken by Yukon residents.

This harvest has, for the most part, been well received in the Yukon. Many residents enjoy the meat and the opportunity to participate in this extraordinary wilderness hunting opportunity. First Nations now again harvest some wood bison, a meat harvest which serves, to a limited extent, to compensate for the costs borne by the community. More importantly, it provides for a growing sense of 'ownership' of the herd. The bison hunt is also important because it gets people out on the land during a season when they are normally not hunting.

Conservation hunting is working to limit the population growth of the herd. This, in turn, keeps the herd within the tolerable social carrying capacity as established by the local people. As such, local communities are more comfortable having re-introduced bison on the land. Perhaps more importantly, conservation hunting appears to be an important means of reconnecting a people with a species that has been long absent.

Wood bison are slowly weaving their way back into the cultural fabric of Yukoners. Many Yukon hunters, having learned about and hunted wood bison, have a new respect and value for the species. This is the most important long-term conservation gain of the hunt—and one that, ultimately, will likely create the public will required to maintain bison on the land. The success of conservation hunting as a management tool for wood bison in the Yukon will be measured over time by changing attitudes regarding the value of wood bison to local peoples. To date, this management approach has served to benefit both co-management and educational goals. As such, this conservation-hunting model has served to realize one of the key goals of comprehensive land claims in the Yukon.

This is the abstract of a formal paper to be submitted for publication in a professional journal. For more information, contact Graham Van Tighem at gvantighem@yknet.ca

Managing Polar Bear Sport Hunting in Nunavut, Canada

Drikus Gissing
Department of Environment
Government of Nunavut, Pond Inlet

Introduction

Sport hunters in Nunavut are categorized as either resident or non-resident sport hunters. At the present time, resident sport hunters must have lived in Nunavut for two years, although new regulations will reduce the residency period to three months. Resident sport hunters must meet all regulatory requirements for a hunting license and are bound by quotas, seasons, and other restrictions on taking the various species.

Any person who is not a resident of Nunavut may be classed as a non-resident sport hunter. Non-resident hunters must apply to hunt through a licensed outfitter and must be taken on the hunt by a licensed guide. All other regulatory requirements must also be satisfied (e.g., obtaining a license and tag indicating the bear is officially allocated by the local community authority, and pay the specified trophy fee).

Managing Sport Hunting in Nunavut

Polar bear is only one of several sport-hunted species taken in Nunavut. The average number of trophies taken in recent years include about 75 polar bears, 120 caribou, 55 muskox, 15-20 walrus, six grizzly bear, five wolves, and two wolverine.

Almost one-third of the global population of polar bear is found in Nunavut. The Nunavut bears are well-managed and protected from unsustainable use. The basis of this successful management program is sound research, strict quotas, and effective monitoring.

In regard to research, the goal is to ensure that each of the 12 regional populations of polar bears occurring in Nunavut is studied every 15 years in order to determine the population size and composition. Quotas are set for each of these regional populations, and a Memorandum of Understanding in regard to these quotas are signed with each community-based Hunters' and Trappers' Organization (HTO). Monitoring programs are in place to ensure that each bear killed is documented and is subtracted from the community quota. Biological samples are taken (e.g., for aging purposes), and tattoos from earlier research encounters and other information are recorded. Export and CITES permits are issued, and the Wildlife Officer in each community works closely with the HTO to monitor and satisfy all requirements for an accurate record of wildlife harvesting activities. In regard to the polar bear hunt, records extend back 30 years on all bears hunted in Nunavut.

Economic Benefits

Polar bears provide the greatest economic value among the various species hunted in Nunavut. Guides, hunt assistants, and tag holders (who may chose to transfer their polar bear tag to a sport hunter) receive 54 percent of the revenues obtained from polar bear sport hunters, with outfitters receiving 22 percent of the total. Provisioning the hunt, providing accommodations, clothing and souvenir sales (in the community) accounts for an additional 13 percent. Flights to the community (7 percent) and government-required trophy and license fees (4 percent) are the only costs that do not directly benefit local community members.

External Factors Affecting the Sport Hunt

The single factor that most impacts the Nunavut sport hunt is the *U.S. Marine Mammal Protection Act* (MMPA). This is because U.S. hunters can only take trophies into the U.S. if they fully satisfy all requirements set down in the MMPA. These requirements include:

- That a monitored and enforced sport-hunting program, consistent with the international polar bear agreement, is in place;

- The program must be based on scientifically-sound quotas that ensure the hunted population is maintained at a sustainable level;
- Trophy exports from Canada into the U.S. are consistent with the provisions of CITES (the *Convention on International Trade in Endangered Species*) and other international conventions;
- The exports and imports are unlikely to contribute to illegal trade in bear parts;
- For those populations shared between jurisdictions (say Canada and Greenland), enforceable science-based management regimes must also be in place.

Based upon information provided by the Nunavut Territorial Government, the U.S. Fish and Wildlife Service in 1994 was satisfied that five (of the 12) Nunavut polar bear populations met the criteria for approval under the MMPA. Once this approval was obtained, sport hunting of polar bears in Nunavut increased by 67 percent, from an average of 45 to 75 hunts per year. In regard to the five approved populations, the number of sport hunts increased 89 percent following the 1994 U.S. decision.

Client Demand for the Hunt

Although the MMPA rulings only affect U.S hunters, this change in sport-hunting activity illustrates the significance of the U.S. client base as a source of hunters for Nunavut outfitters, guides, and communities. This is because U.S. hunters are the easiest for booking agents to access, they represent the largest pool of potential clients worldwide, and they are generally prepared to pay more for the hunt. The loss or restriction of this client base would have a significant negative impact on the Nunavut economy.

Thus for those polar bear populations approved under the MMPA, 92 percent of hunters are from the U.S., with 6 percent from Europe and the remainder from Canada and Asia. For those polar bear populations not approved under the MMPA, the hunters come from a larger variety of countries, although 34 percent of these hunters continue to come from the U.S. The remainder originate from Europe (37 percent), South America (12 percent), Canada (10 percent), Asia (4 percent), Australasia (2 percent), and Africa (1 percent).

Expanding the Hunt

Among the Nunavut regional polar bear populations not approved under the MMPA, the next likely candidate population for approval is the Gulf of Boothia population. Research findings recently completed by the Government of Nunavut indicate that the population appears to be in good health and is capable of sustaining current, or even increased, levels of hunting. Approval of the Gulf of Boothia population is currently being considered by the U.S. Fish and Wildlife Service based on information provided by the Government of Nunavut and the Canadian Polar Bear Technical Committee. Approval under the MMPA for the Gulf of Boothia population could provide significant economic benefits to the communities hunting polar bears in this region of Nunavut.

In order to ensure that Nunavut polar bear sport hunts satisfy the requirements set out in the MMPA, the Government of Nunavut must:

- Maintain its commitment to polar bear research and management;
- Continue to work with its co-management partners, including the HTOs, Regional Wildlife Organizations [RWOs], and the Nunavut Wildlife Management Board [NWMB] to ensure quotas remain within sustainable limits;
- Establish co-management agreements with neighboring jurisdictions/nations sharing polar bear populations with Nunavut (discussions leading to such co-management agreements are currently being initiated).

Conclusions

Despite the overall success of science-based management of polar bears in Nunavut, some challenges remain, or may appear in the future. For example, there remains the challenge of having Inuit traditional knowledge (*Inuit qaujimajatuqangit* [IQ]) appropriately incorporated into polar bear management. In the future, there may be challenges to some provisions of the *Nunavut Wildlife Act* (as some southern-based outfitters are looking for loopholes in the requirement that dog-teams be used in all sport hunts).

Nevertheless, at the present time, it is widely acknowledged that polar bear management in Nunavut is a success story, insofar as research and IQ have demonstrated that most polar bear populations have increased in size, to the point where high polar bear numbers in some locations have become a threat to public safety.

Trophy Hunting of Mountain Ungulates: Opportunities and Pitfalls

Marco Festa-Bianchet
Département de biologie
Université de Sherbrooke,Québec

Introduction

Trophy hunting of mountain ungulates targets mature male animals with large horns. The hunt involves a 'competitive' component, in that trophies are 'scored,' with high-scoring horns more highly valued than lower-scoring horns.

Trophy hunters pay large sums for the opportunity to obtain a trophy—for mountain sheep typically $15,000 – 35,000 per hunt. In some countries, the majority of trophy hunters are non-resident, and so the tourism revenues generated from such hunts are valued, both in local communities and by governments. Over the past decade, there has been a great expansion of trophy hunts for several species of mountain ungulates in Asian countries.

Threats and Benefits Associated with Trophy Hunting

As hunters generally seek mature (larger-horned) males, this form of hunting should have a minor effect on population growth. Instead, major threats to the conservation of mountain ungulates in several Asian countries include:

- Competition, for grazing land, from domestic livestock;
- Exotic diseases;
- Habitat destruction;
- Poaching for meat and commercial products.

There are several potential conservation benefits associated with trophy hunting, including:

- Revenues for habitat protection, anti-poaching measures, and public education;
- Funding for research, monitoring, and management programs;
- Realized value of wildlife (the economic value each live animal represents);
- Incentive to protect the habitat of the hunted populations.

Currently however, a small minority of mountain-ungulate trophy-hunting programs can claim to have a positive impact on conservation. The hunts for markhor and urial carried out in Torghar (in Pakistan) have a clear benefit for conservation, while the argali and blue sheep hunts in Aksai, Gansu (China) only have a minor positive effect on local conservation.

In the latter case, although the fee for each argali hunt is $21,500, less than 5 percent of that sum is used for conservation purposes. If the program was improved, it could generate about $60,000 for conservation. Livestock overgrazing represents an unresolved threat to argali in this region.

An apparent failure appears to be the argali hunt in Mongolia, where there is little evidence that any funds generated from the hunt are used for conservation. In 2002, the number of hunting permits doubled (from 40 to 80 in number). Argali populations in Mongolia have declined by 75-80 percent over the past 25 years.

In the Mongolian example, all the trophy-hunt outfitters are based in the capital (none in the hunting districts), and the local governments report losing money as a result of the argali hunts. As a result of these unfortunate outcomes, there is reported to be increasing local opposition to trophy hunting in the region.

The 'take home message' from these Asian experiences includes the following:

- Although there is great potential for conservation—and local economic—benefits, at the present time, these benefits are not always realized;
- Although much is said and promised about 'conservation hunts,' in reality most hunts are purely commercial operations;
- The impact on conservation of most trophy hunting programs is nil or slightly negative;
- Trophy hunts may increase the potential for artificial selection to negatively affect the hunted populations.

Does Trophy Hunting have a Negative Impact on Mountain Ungulate Populations?

Males with the largest horns are targeted by trophy hunting. Large horns are a product of age, food availability, and genetics (larger-horned fathers will tend to produce large-horned sons). In Alberta, a bighorn sheep with large horns will have high mating success when between 7 – 8 years old, but runs a high risk of being shot when 4 – 6 years of age, before his large horns can have a positive effect on his mating success.

Given this selective pressure being exerted by trophy hunters on breeding males, the genetic component (the 'breeding value') of both horn length and body weight was found to decline significantly over a 30-year period subject to trophy-hunters' selective removal of large-horned animals. For each ungulate species, it is important to determine the age-specific mortality pattern, because this can vary substantially among species (see Figure 1). In species with high survival, such as ibex, trophy hunting targeted at younger age classes should lead to a greater deviation from the 'normal' age structure.

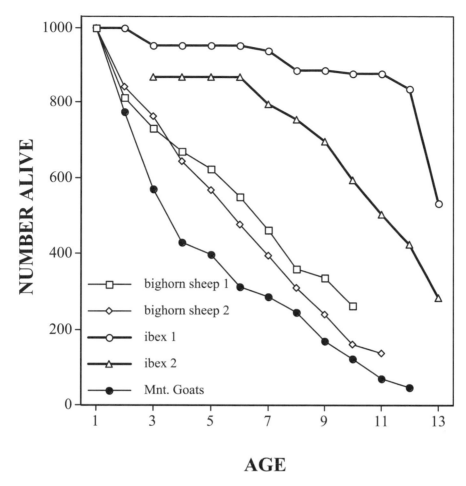

Figure 1. Survival of a cohort of 1000 yearling males in two populations of bighorn sheep (Ram Mountain [1], and Sheep River [2]) and one of mountain goats in Alberta, and two populations of Alpine ibex (Belledonne, France, and Levionaz, Italy).

Conclusions

In the case of mountain ungulates, there appears to be a risk of artificial selection affecting the fitness of hunted populations where trophy value is based on the size of the breeding animals' horns. However, more research on the basic biology will be required before definitive management advice can be provided on this matter.

Claims of conservation benefit of trophy hunting are rarely realized; there is a disconnect between the potential benefits, the realized benefits, and the rhetoric.

Acknowledgements

Thanks are due to students Steeve Côté, Fanie Pelletier, Kathreen Ruckstuhl, Mylène Leblanc, Achaz von Hardenberg, and collaborators Jean-Michel Gaillard, David Coltman, Wendy King, Tim Coulson, Jon Jorgenson, Jack Hogg and Bill Wishart. The Natural Sciences & Engineering Research Council of Canada, Fonds FQRNT (Québec) and the Alberta Research Council provided financial support for this research.

Designing Hunting and Wildlife Programs to Enhance the Sustainability of Northern Communities

Barney Smith and Harvey Jessup
Fish and Wildlife Branch, Department of Environment
Government of Yukon, Whitehorse

Introduction

When we design hunting and wildlife programs, we usually consider what needs to be done (activities) to meet objectives for harvest, habitat, and populations. An alternative approach is to think about 'desired outcomes' and the long-term sustainability of communities, because this helps to define the future we want and prepare for futures that may be likely.

There are six reasons why northern wildlife co-management partners need to think about the long-term sustainability of communities when they design hunting and wildlife programs.

- The sustainability of communities is very important to families, businesses, and governments for many economic, social, and cultural reasons.
- Local families and businesses may not be getting the benefits they should from nearby wildlife populations.
- Having lots of people at meetings and dealing with the concerns they raise does not guarantee that we are doing enough to make communities more sustainable.
- Current wildlife priorities are often short-term, reactive, and assume other programs are dealing with community sustainability.
- It is important to find ways to address the bleak outlook on the future that is becoming common, particularly in Elders, in discussions about climate change.
- There are many changes such as climate and technology affecting wildlife, hunting, and communities that may combine to reduce long-term sustainability.

This paper looks at six dimensions of community sustainability and their associated desired outcomes that hunting and wildlife programs can incorporate to help northern communities be more sustainable.

Community Sustainability

Thinking about community sustainability can be quite complicated because we use the term sustainability in many ways, and because hunting and wildlife programs only contribute in part to what is required for a northern community to be sustainable. However, hunters in seven arctic communities in northwest Canada and northeast Alaska came up with some practical definitions.[1] Based on their ideas, we look at six dimensions to helping northern communities be more sustainable that co-management partners need to consider when they design and evaluate hunting and wildlife programs. As far as wildlife and hunting are concerned, a northern community may be more sustainable over the long term when:

- Local families and businesses feel direct economic benefits from adjacent wildlife;
- The sustenance economy is strong;
- Hunting cultural values are widespread in adults and youth;
- People feel a sense of local control and ownership in wildlife decisions;
- Local families experience wellness in its many dimensions;
- Local families and businesses are more able to cope with changes they need to make related to wildlife and hunting.

Some possible outcomes to aim for in our plans for hunting and wildlife programs, in each of these six dimensions, are listed below.

---

[1] Kofinas, G.P., and S. R. Braund. 1996. Defining Arctic Community Sustainability: A background paper prepared for the NSF Sustainability of Arctic Communities Project. 12 pp.
(http://www.taiga.net/sustain/lib/reports/sustainability.html)

Direct economic benefits. Social outcomes that could lead to direct economic benefits to local families and businesses include:

- Rental and service income from hunters, wildlife viewers and other wild-area users;
- Allocation of commercial hunting opportunities are seen to be fair;
- Hosting peer exchanges of hunters from regions to the North who are preparing for climate change;
- Income to families and expenditures with businesses keeping important habitats in good condition;
- Income from the sale of certain tissues and crafts;
- Income from hunting stories told to or written for visitors and others;
- Youth feeling that guiding and trapping are attractive lifestyles and seasonal work;
- Local hire by regional businesses that depend on wildlife and wild areas.

Strong sustenance economies. Social outcomes that could lead to strong sustenance economies of local families and businesses include:

- High skill levels and respectful hunting by all hunters;
- Organized meat sharing;
- Organized trail systems where some local trails are secret;
- Places where older people can safely camp for several weeks where family members can visit and hunt;
- Allocation that allows for meat needs of local communities and guiding businesses to be met;
- Knowledgeable, skilled and organized meat collectors hunting for relatives in a sustainable manner;
- Reports on the social and economic importance of the sustenance economy;
- Reduced feelings that reporting wildlife declines will inevitably lead to imposed restrictions on hunting;

- Annual gatherings where hunters can learn about patterns in how many wildlife are taken by hunters in various areas and how the wildlife are faring;
- Local lobbying for policies and guidelines that meet local needs.

Continuing hunting culture and values. Leadership and design by aboriginal governments is essential. The social outcomes that could maintain and enhance hunting cultures and values include:

- Seasonal camps where youth learn from elders;
- School hunts and on-the-land school work about wildlife;
- Safe access for families to culturally-significant camps;
- Trials of traditional hunt-management systems;
- Write-ups about important family connections to places that describe what the places and wildlife were like at various times;
- Celebrations of culturally-significant harvesting activities;
- Low levels of fear about the risks of sharing culturally-significant ideas;
- Culturally-relevant training of hunters and guides;
- Widespread attention to proper ways of behaving on the land;
- Intercept-training of hunting parties on the land by Elders and patrollers.

Local control over wildlife decisions. Social outcomes that could lead to greater local control over wildlife decisions include:

- Families and businesses participating in effective consultation procedures;
- Individuals who are knowledgeable about wildlife feeling their ideas are valued and their time sharing those ideas has been well used;
- Local experience and skills in helping the community decide on its agenda and moving this forward;

- Easier implementation of 2–3 year trials of ideas from communities where the goals are improvement, learning and trust-building—not perfection;
- High levels of trust between individuals involved in co-management, even if between-party trust is not what it could be;
- Well-informed formal and informal community leaders participating in planning;
- Local understanding of the potential impacts of all studies;
- Patrolling that demonstrates low levels of cheating, poaching, and unsustainable hunting;
- Properly functioning bodies set up after land claims that are well-informed and whose recommendations are respected;
- People in communities and representatives on land claim bodies having informed opinions based on views on sustainability from the community and elsewhere, and, with trained facilitation, develop their own model of conservation hunting that suits their situation.

Wellness. Social outcomes that could lead to enhanced wellness include:

- Family members of all ages and body shapes active in a range of hunting-related activities over many months each year;
- Patrollers available to provide emergency and other support to Elders and less-able hunters;
- Land-based healing activities;
- Community feasts and other celebrations involving wild meat;
- Safe hunt plans that account for new risks and unexpected weather;
- Families consuming healthy country foods with known and negligible toxin levels;
- Hunting regulations that emphasize participation opportunities.

Increased resilience to change. Social outcomes that increase resilience to change in local hunting systems include:

- Frequent gatherings where hunters and others can exchange ideas with scientists about how the land and wildlife are changing, and what to pay attention to;
- Local understanding that change is often sudden, surprising, and subtle;
- Support to help wildlife-related businesses change to adapt to new climate situations rather than economic subsidies to help them get by;
- Hunters sharing what they learned while hunting in new places, especially farther south, with local hunters there;
- Local understanding that it is important to report unusual phenomena;
- Hunting new species that are introduced or move north;
- Local understanding of wildlife diseases and reporting;
- Good 'what-if' thinking skills in hunters and others;
- Experiments where people try new ways of making a living from wildlife;
- Plans for areas that will be important for many different kinds of wildlife, even as the climate changes;
- High levels of empathy for families stressed by change, and lower levels of cynicism, blaming, and criticism.

Moving Ahead

It will be hard to choose which outcomes to achieve first. Governments usually focus on economic benefits as part of their job creation agenda. It may be effective to try different ideas and share experiences so we learn faster. This will require more flexibility in how hunting rules are made, greater open-mindedness to new ideas, and faster ways of making decisions. We need to be careful what situations are called a 'crisis' as resources get trapped there. We need to involve people who know about the social side of communities and what really helps them become more sustainable. Finally, we need to tap into the money governments currently spend on enhancing community sustainability that currently fund job creation and new infrastructure.

Note

Papers in preparation discuss these ideas in more detail. They look at social outcomes in collaboratively designed wildlife programs and how to enhance community sustainability through wildlife programs and policies. These papers will be available on the website www.yfwmb.ca/co-management. Please email inquiries to Barney.Smith@gov.yk.ca

Break-Out Groups Reports

Group A: Is the Selective Hunting of Trophy Males a Problem?

Elders have expressed concern that the selective removal of larger males may cause problems for the animal population. Biologists agree that removing these dominant individuals may affect the reproductive success of the stock, but the degree to which this occurs is not well understood and is probably different for each species.

Removing large male animals can affect the population in two main ways. The first is through genetic impact, because larger males father larger and competitively-advantaged male offspring. The second is behavioral and ecological if, or when, these older, stronger animals serve important purposes, e.g., when making trails or digging through snow to uncover forage, actions that will provide benefits to younger or smaller members of the population. Concerns of Elders also extend to solitary animals like polar bears, where removal of dominant males determines the future characteristics of individuals in the population.

Does removing the larger trophy animals create any other problems, e.g., for outfitters or guides? Again, for Aboriginal guides and outfitters in particular (but also for some non-Aboriginal outfitters operating in or from Aboriginal communities), the opinions of community Elders can have an important influence on their business operations. Governments may also place restrictions on trophy hunting for these, and also for safety, reasons.

Animals of different size and age may have different economic value, either in regard to the quantity or quality of meat and fat they provide, but also the price and saleability of the different-sized hides. For example, in some cases the largest hides are harder to sell and therefore fetch a lower price.

Hunters attitudes may change under market pressures; there may be pressure from peers or clients to take the largest animals, and outfitters in particular are susceptible to such pressures. In addition, the trophy hunter may have little concern for the long-term welfare of the hunted population, whereas the local community will be acutely aware and responsive to the continuing existence of those resources.

However, communities, as well as guides and outfitters, benefit from the revenues that trophy hunters bring to the community, so that compromises may be acceptable. In cases where taking larger trophy males is a concern, the subsistence hunters can attempt to balance any disadvantages associated with this practice by taking more female and younger male animals for their own purposes.

Group B: Who Decides What can be Hunted?

A number of different groups influence, and in some cases can determine, the extent of permissible hunting of a given species-population. The local community, although vitally interested in that management decision, may exert a relatively minor influence (in some cases, perhaps only 25 percent) on that final decision. Other influences are exerted by various levels of government (including foreign governments), the scientific community, and special interest groups in the general public. In total, these non-local influences may greatly outweigh the local influences on management decisions.

The local or user-community, through appropriate local institutions (e.g., councils, Hunters' and Trappers' Organizations, etc.) is able to make its' views known to management bodies at the regional or national level. Communities, through prepared reports, resolutions or petitions, and by sending delegates to participate in management meetings outside the community, can inform and influence management decisions that are important to the community. The resource users, at the community level, may have important information that is unknown to outside decision-makers, e.g., information on long-term population trends, or local-level environmental changes.

Researchers, carrying out their work in association with user-communities, can in some cases help influence the management decision-making process. This can be done by preparing reports that reflect and reinforce community knowledge and concerns in a more formal (and hence advantageous) documentary manner than may otherwise be available to the community.

On the other hand, some scientists may present their own conclusions in reports—conclusions that contradict the community consensus. In cases where little scientific information exists on a particular wildlife population, such contrary views can have, from the community's point of view, a decidedly negative impact on the management decision.

Other non-local constraints that may influence management decisions include various administrative/legislative policies imposed by foreign governments (e.g., the U.S. *Marine Mammal Protection Act* [MMPA]) or positions these governments take at international meetings (e.g., CITES).

In many instances today, the Canadian (federal) Government shares management responsibility with provincial/territorial governments, or has further devolved management responsibilities to regional decision-making bodies. Where co-management boards have been established, management decision-making may be most responsive to the concerns of resource users. However, in some cases (especially where the species or populations may be considered threatened or otherwise 'at risk'), federal legislation (e.g, the *Species at Risk Act* in Canada; the *Endangered Species Act* in other countries) may tilt decision-making away from responsiveness to local concerns and knowledge.

There is still considerable international pressure exerted on local communities. There is a need for more internal consensus before effective action can be taken. The incorporation of traditional ecological knowledge (TEK) serves to empower local communities, even though some problems remain in doing this in respect to hunting regulations. Problems include the adequacy of documenting TEK, and that TEK and western scientists collect data differently. However, despite these difficulties, TEK can contribute a critical context for interpreting and applying scientific data.

Group C: What is the Future of Hunting?

A number of factors may negatively impact the future of hunting. These include habitat loss, species decline, economic forces, public opinion and international pressures against hunting, climate change, introduction of alien species, land use conflicts, and the declining participation of youth in hunting. This last concern exists in the North as well as in southern societies.

In regard to the social conditions that may affect the future of hunting in the North, a number of actions can be taken. A Northern Youth Strategy that encourages an active interest in hunting among young people needs further development. Such a strategy should stress that community and family members serve as important role models to youth. It should include a mentorship program so that young people have every opportunity to experience and learn about hunting from skilled individuals. It is also helpful if academic credit could be given by the schools for the time students spend learning skills on the land. Knowledge that Elders possess about the animals, travel, safety and survival techniques, medicines, and associated knowledge and attitudes needed for hunting competence should be transmitted to young people. The importance of hands-on experience is very important.

A number of strategies can be considered to educate youth living outside the North about hunting. Such activities should provide information that counters the sometimes biased information that urban youth are exposed to and that may incline them to view hunting as an anachronism. At a quite basic level, urban students need to be made aware, and experience, how nutritious food is obtained from the land, that agriculture and fish farms are not the only means of producing animal protein, and that wildlife harvesting and hunting are legitimate and beneficial forms of land use. For schoolroom teaching to be an important tool, teachers must have access to appropriate, unbiased, information for classroom use.

Mentorship and hunter-education programs are especially important for urban youth, for many have no opportunity to hunt with a family member or friend. Consequently, organizations such as Hunter Education Instructors' Associations can play an important role in youth education.

> *For in the end we will only conserve what we love*
> *We will only love what we understand*
> *And we will only understand what we are taught*
> (Baba Dioum, African Conservationist)

Group D: How can Hunters Better Protect their Interests?

The present weakness in the hunting community is that although there are many 'little voices,' there is no unified or common voice. Although hunters may be represented by an organization at the national level in various countries, there is no appropriate representation made by these various national organizations at meetings of various international regulatory bodies (e.g., at CITES).

Although hunters and wildlife harvesters work for the same goal, they do not appear to effectively communicate among themselves. An example here was the absence of hunters' voices from across Canada supporting hunters in British Columbia when BC hunters were fighting to protect a grizzly bear hunt in their region.

Hunters need to make better political and educational use of their strengths, including their knowledge of the contributions hunters have made and continue to make to recovery of depleted wildlife populations, habitat reclamation and protection, and other conservation activities. The hunting community possesses competence in conservation, and many outfitters are concerned and knowledgeable about land and resources and the threats to the integrity of both.

The public must appreciate that hunting is an important component of the ancient and continuing cultural heritage of many peoples throughout the world. They must understand the economic and recreational benefits derived from hunting in rural and less-developed regions of the world.

Hunting organizations exist to advise and assist others. For example, CIC-International Council for Game and Wildlife Conservation can provide assistance with networking and outreach. Although based in Europe, CIC has members worldwide, and many active commissions, working groups and projects. (www.cic-wildlife.org)

This Edmonton conference should be repeated, to continue the discussions and networking, perhaps every two years on a regular basis. Such meetings can certainly serve to bring together key players from across Canada in order to increase exchange of ideas and offer support to communities or regional organizations that seek advice and other assistance.

Open Discussion Following the Break-Out Groups' Reports

A number of useful fora provide information exchange among hunting organizations. For example, FACE, which represents all hunting organizations, convenes meetings where about 40 leading hunting organizations can meet to consider important issues.

There is a Governors' and Premiers' Symposium, often involving about 1,000 people. Clearly this is a politically-important meeting. At the regional level, groups meet to discuss issues relevant to hunters everywhere; e.g., the British Columbia Guide and Outfitters Association discussed the image of hunting at a recent annual meeting.

It was suggested that at a future meeting, consideration could be given to discussing the barren-ground caribou hunts, as this Edmonton meeting was not the forum to consider all the impacts of concern in the North.

The Director of Wildlife from the Nunavut organization representing land claim beneficiaries, expressed his organization's support for a proposed resolution in support of immediately lifting an unwarranted ban on polar bear trophy hunting in the central Canadian Arctic. This action was justified now that the Canadian management authorities were satisfied that several years of research had demonstrated the recovery of a formerly depleted polar bear population in that region, and the importance to small Inuit communities in the region of reinstating these trophy hunts.

Participants recognized that self-determination and following agreed-upon administrative procedure is important to the Inuit. Therefore, in the polar bear case, lack of action at the international level after Canadian Inuit and government actions to research and assist in the recovery of a depleted population was considered very regrettable. The call for a conference resolution in support of lifting the polar bear hunting ban did not receive unanimous support. However, what was deemed acceptable was a petition by the Inuit community-based wildlife organizations, calling for a lifting of the import ban, signed by senior elected Inuit wildlife officials attending the conference. This signed communication, omitting any reference to the conference, will be transmitted to the relevant foreign government authorities whose inaction was the cause of the concern being expressed.

The Chair of the IUCN Sustainable Use Specialist Group offered an organizational affiliation with IUCN-World Conservation Union for a North American specialist group focused upon conservation hunting. This action, by IUCN, provides additional legitimacy to conservation-hunting programs and will be acted upon by a core group participating in the Edmonton conference (see report on the focus group discussion on conference follow-up actions, below).

Focus Group Discussion on Follow-Up Actions

At the conclusion of the conference, a small focus-group of conference participants discussed how to usefully continue working on conservation-hunting best practices and how to sustain the useful dialogue that occurred during the conference. There was awareness that many in the conservation-hunting constituency had been unable to participate in this conference, and as a consequence of this, the task of completing a compendium of conservation-hunting best practices required more work.

To assist in this task, a proposal was made by Jon Hutton, Chair of the IUCN Sustainable Use Specialist Groups' program. This proposal was that following the recent dissolution of the IUCN-North American Sustainable Use Specialists' Group [IUCN North American-SUSG], a new North American-SUSG be constituted, based at the University of Alberta, with its program focus being *Conservation Hunting.*

During discussion of this suggestion, the following tentative list of tasks to be undertaken by the new SUSG was proposed:

- Take steps to establish a new political narrative called 'conservation hunting'
  Although hunting is a legitimate and powerful conservation tool, it has to overcome negative (public) perceptions that some associate with such current terms as, e.g., 'sport-', 'trophy-' and 'recreational-hunting.'

- Unambiguously and comprehensively define the term *Conservation Hunting*
  This is necessary to ensure the term *conservation hunting* cannot be co-opted, corrupted or otherwise misunderstood and misused by others.

It is important to be clear, when referring to 'benefits' (related to, e.g., conservation, rural economic development, cultural and social reinforcement in indigenous and local communities) derived from conservation hunting programs, just what these diverse benefits are.

- **Develop and promote conservation-hunting best practices**
  These best practices will be derived from case studies, and are required to be made evident, so that transparency accompanies the promotion of conservation hunting as a conservation tool.

- **Assess the possibility of a future need to consider hunter 'certification'**
  Looking to the future, there may be a time when certification of hunting (especially where it provides 'commercial' benefits) is demanded or becomes politically useful (as a pre-emptive action taken to safeguard conservation hunting programs against unwarranted actions by opponents of conservation hunting). In anticipation of such a need arising, those promoting conservation hunting should be ready to take the lead in any such certification initiative taken by opponents.

- **Overcoming resistance and 'putting our house in order'**
  It may be necessary to consider some formal arrangements to ensure that a network of knowledgeable practitioners can work together effectively to defend conservation hunting as a practice. There may be resistance to the very notion of conservation hunting by some activist groups who see sustainable use/conservation-hunting programs as being antagonistic to their own wildlife protection activities.

- **Addressing the question of eco-tourism**
  Eco-tourism is being promoted by some as a good conservation measure because, e.g., it increases public awareness of the plight of endangered species and the beauty/importance/intrinsic value of the natural world. To

some, and especially those who oppose the consumptive use of wildlife, eco-tourism is promoted as a panacea, the silver bullet that will provide financial resources that remove the need of impoverished rural peoples to kill animals in order to sustain themselves.

The differences, and relationship, between eco-tourism (that only 'shoots' wildlife with cameras) and conservation-hunting programs, needs to be made explicit. This may be undertaken by assembling reliable data comparing the revenue streams generated by each activity, and the conservation, environmental, and social impacts associated with wildlife viewing and wildlife hunting.

- **Bringing conservation hunting into mainstream conservation thinking**
  This can be accomplished by promoting research, conferences/workshops, publications and improved outreach/extension programs (see below) that focus upon conservation-hunting programs.

- **Extension activities**
  Workshops, hunter-education/mentorship programs, discussions with civic and youth groups, and other forms of extension (using film, mass media, school curricula, public speaking engagements—especially to teachers' groups) need to be developed and used as a means of demonstrating the benefits for wildlife, people, and the environment of responsible conservation-hunting programs.

- **Regulation and market development**
  Involvement of the hunting industry in these discussions will ensure that conservation-hunting programs are conducted in as rational and defensible a manner as possible.

However, as conservation hunting as a term and as an activity becomes better known, so is the threat to such programs likely to increase as a result of greater re-action of opponents to the increased public awareness of such programs.

To promote and market conservation-hunting programs, it will be necessary to ensure that they are:

o   appropriately regulated,
o   effectively monitored,
o   demonstrably sustainable,
o   humane, through the use of appropriate weapons in the hands of competent (i.e., experienced, or supervised) hunters (see below).

Thought should be given to needed regulation, business sustainability issues, and addressing possible/likely future certification issues (see above).

- **Questions relating to 'humaneness' of hunting**
  As nations become increasingly urbanized, so animal welfare and animal rights lobbies and legislation will likely demand that hunting meets progressively more stringent criteria of 'humaneness.' Some recent measures already being used to place obstacles in the way of wildlife users include:

  o   Idealized goals, such as instantaneous death (or at the very least, instant unconsciousness) are now demanded in whaling (by aboriginal hunters) for example, with increasing attention paid to 'time to death' (a proxy measure for 'suffering') after the projectile enters the body. Whaling nations are now required to conduct extensive and expensive research on ballistics and pathology, and to replace conventional weapons with newly-developed (and in some cases, prohibitively expensive) equipment.

  o   Requiring ongoing research to develop more and more 'humane' traps, so that as these new traps are developed, expensive trap replacement and training programs become required.

o Questions about crippling rates (in wildfowl) in some jurisdictions are proving problematic for hunters.

- **What animals are to be included under conservation-hunting programs?**
  Do conservation-hunting programs include marine species (e.g., marine sport fish, such as marlin, swordfish?) and marine mammals (walrus?), or does conservation hunting only encompass terrestrial or four-footed wildlife? Where are waterfowl in relation to this definition, and exotic or non-native animals on enclosed private lands? Does the term conservation hunting only apply to hunting native species— whether terrestrial or marine—in their natural habitat (i.e., in-situ hunting)?

APPENDIX I: CONFERENCE PROGRAM

People, Wildlife & Hunting: Emerging Conservation Paradigms

Thursday, 21 October 2004, Evening:

6.00 – 8.00   ACA-sponsored Welcoming Reception

Friday, 22 October, Morning:

9.00   Chair: Milton Freeman (CCI, U of A)
             Opening remarks
9.10   Shane Mahoney (Environment & Conservation
             Department, Newfoundland & Labrador)
             *The Challenge of Wildlife Management: A Multicultural
             Perspective*
9.30   William Wall (Conservation Biologist, Virginia, USA)
             Key Components of Successful C-H Programs
10.00   Peter J. Ewins (WWF-Canada, Toronto)
             Conservation & Hunting in Northern Regions
10.25   Coffee
10.50   Panel: *Community Perspectives on Conservation-
             Hunting Programs.*
             Grand Chief Herb Norwegian (Deh Cho First Nations,
             Fort Simpson, NT)
             James Pokiak (Ookpik Tours & Adventures,
             Tuktoyaktuk, NT)
             Joyce Rabesca (Tli Cho Outfitters, Rae, NT)
             Moise Rabesca (Tli Cho Outfitters, Rae, NT)
             Harry Smith (Champagne-Aishinik First Nation, Haines
             Junction, YT)
11.40   Open Discussion
12.15   Lunch

Friday, Afternoon

             Chair: Lee Foote (ACCRU, U of A)
1.30   Panel: *Economic/Marketing, Policy, and
             Social/Attitudinal Constraints & Challenges.*
             Sylvia Birkholz (Alberta Sustainable Resource
             Development)

	Naomi Krogman (Rural Sociology, University of Alberta)
	Marty Luckert (Rural Economy, University of Alberta)
	Kelly Semple (Hunting for Tomorrow Foundation)
2.15	Open discussion
2.45	Session: *Examples of Successful Conservation-Hunting Programs*
	Jon Hutton (IUCN-SUSG, Cambridge)
	A Global Perspective: Examples from Africa and Elsewhere
3.10	Coffee break
3.40	George Wenzel (Human Geography, McGill University)
	Polar Bear C-H Programs in Arctic Canada: Benefits and Challenges
4.05	Dean Cluff (NWT Resources, Economic Development & Wildlife)
	The NWT Barren-ground Caribou Sport Hunt
4.30	Frank Pokiak (Inuvialuit Game Council, Inuvik)
	Co-management and Conservation Hunting in the Western Canadian Arctic
4.55	Open Discussion
5.15	Adjourn

Friday, Evening:

7.30-8.30	Films and Informal Discussion

Saturday, 23 October, Morning:

	Chair: Robert Hudson (ACCRU, U of A)
9.00	Kai Wollscheid (CIC-International Council for Game and Wildlife Management)
	Multilateral Environmental Agreements and the Future of Hunting
9.25	Session: *Initiating and Managing Successful C-H Programs*
	Lee Foote (Alberta Cooperative Conservation Research Unit)
	Principles and Progress in Regard to Sustainable C-H Programs
9.40	Graham Van Tighem (Yukon Fish & Wildlife Management Board)

	The Wood Bison Conservation-hunting Program in Yukon
10.05	Drikus Gissing (Nunavut Department of Environment) *Managing Conservation-hunting Programs in the Canadian Eastern Arctic*
10.30	Coffee break
11.00	Marco Festa-Bianchet (IUCN-SSC, University of Sherbrooke) *Trophy Hunting of Mountain Ungulates: Opportunities and Pitfalls*
11.25	Barney Smith (Yukon Department of Environment) *Recent Yukon Experiences with Commercial and Family-based Hunting Systems: Implications for Conservation Hunting.*
11.50	Open discussion
12.15	Lunch

Saturday Afternoon:

	Chair: Milton Freeman (CCI, U of A)
1.30	Break-out sessions: *Does the selective hunting of large trophy males create problems?* *Who decides what can be hunted?* *What is the future of recreational hunting?* *How can hunters best protect their interests?*
3.15	Coffee break
3.45	Reports from Break-out sessions
4.30	Open discussion
5.15	Adjourn

Saturday Evening:

| 6.30 | Conference Banquet |

Sunday, 26 October:

8.30	Leave for Elk Island National Park (Plains & wood bison, moose, deer, elk, etc.) Hunters' Lunch (Bison stew etc.) at the park
1.30	Arrive back at Greenwood Inn
1.45	Focus Group Discussion: Conference follow-up actions.
4.0	Adjourn

List of Registered Participants
People, Wildlife & Hunting Conference, Edmonton, October 2004

Aksawnee, David
Kivalliq Wildlife Board
Box 225
Baker Lake NU, X0C 0A0
Tel: 867-793-2520
Fax: 867-793-2034

Ambrock, Ken
Assistant Deputy Minister
Fish and Wildlife Division
Department of Sustainable
Resource Development
Government of Alberta
9915 – 108 Street, 11th Floor
Edmonton AB, T5K 2G8
Tel: 780-427-6749
Fax: 780-427-8884
Ken.ambrock@gov.ab.ca

Anderson, Robert
Alberta Conservation Association
P.O. Box 40027
Baker Centre Postal Outlet
Edmonton AB, T5J 4M9
Tel: 780-427-5192
Fax: 780-422-6441

Auriat, Denise
Gwich'in Renewable Resources
Board
P.O. Box 2240
Inuvik NT, X0E 0T0
Tel: 867-777-6610
denise.auriat@grrb.nt.ca

Birkholz, Sylvia
Head, Licensing & Revenue
Service
Department of Sustainable
Resource Development
Government of Alberta
9920 – 108 Street, 2nd Floor
Edmonton AB, T5K 2M4
Tel: 780-427-8078
sylvia.birkholz@gov.ab.ca

Bocharnikov, Vladimir
RAIPON–Russian Association of
Indigenous Peoples of the North
Kirov Street 62-322
Vladivostok 690089,
Primorskii krai, Russia
Tel: 7-4232-323651
Fax: 7-4232-312159
vbocharnikov@mail.ru

Boyce, Mark
ACA Chair in Fisheries & Wildlife
Department of Biological
Sciences
University of Alberta
Edmonton AB, T6G 2E9
Tel: 780-492-0081
Fax: 780-492-9234
mark.boyce@ualberta.ca

Bradley, Dale
Co-chair
Selkirk Renewable Resources
Council
Box 32
Pelly Crossing, Yukon Y0B 1P0
Tel: 867-537-3937
Fax: 867-537-3939
franks.bradley@yknet.yk.ca

Brink, Mabel
Alberta Society of Professional
Outfitters
103 – 6030 88 Street
Edmonton AB, T6E 6G4
Tel: 780-414-0249
Fax: 780-465-6801
mabel@apos.ab.ca

Campbell, Ernie
Manager, Wildlife & Environment
North Slave Region
Resources, Wildlife & Economic
Development
Government of the Northwest
Territories
P.O. Box 2668
Yellowknife NT, X1A 2P9
Tel: 867-873-7019
Fax: 867-873-6230
ernie_campbell@govt.nt.ca

Casaway, Modeste
Lutsel K'e First Nation
Box 28
Lutsel K'e NT, X0E 1A0
Tel: 867-370-3197
wildlife@lutselke.com

Cleator, Holly
Department of Fisheries &
Oceans
501 University Crescent
Winnipeg MB, R3T 2N6
Tel: 204-983-8975
Fax: 204-983-5192
cleatorh@dfo-mpo.gc.ca

Cluff, Dean
Regional Biologist, North Slave
Region
Resources, Wildlife & Economic
Development
Government of the Northwest
Territories
P.O. Box 2668
Yellowknife NT, X1A 2P9
Tel: 867-873-7783
Fax: 867-873-6230
dean_cluff@govt.nt.ca

Coltman, David
Department of Biological
Sciences
University of Alberta
Edmonton AB, T6G 2E9
Tel: 780-492-7255
Fax: 780-492-9234
david.coltman@ualberta.ca

Corrigan, Rob
Alberta Conservation Association
P.O. Box 40027
Baker Centre Postal Outlet
Edmonton AB, T5J 4M9
Tel: 780-427-5192
Fax: 780-422-6441

Dean, Bert
Associate Director
Wildlife Department
Nunavut Tunngavik Inc.
Box 280
Rankin Inlet NU, X0C 0G0
Tel: 867-645-5425
Fax: 867-645-3451
bertdean@arctic.ca

Derocher, Andrew
Department of Biological
Sciences
University of Alberta
Edmonton AB, T6G 2E9
Tel: 780-492-5570
Fax: 780-492-9234
derocher@ualberta.ca

Drown, Dale
Guide & Outfitters Association of
BC
Suite 250, 7580 River Road
Richmond BC, V6X 1X6
Tel: 604-278-2688
Fax: 604-278-3440
drown@goabc.org

Drury, Barbara
Laberge Renewable Resources
Council
Box 20723
Whitehorse YK, Y1A 7A2
Tel: 867-668-1045
Fax: 867-393-3950
drury@yt.sympatico.ca

Eberhart, Kevin
Tsuga Forestry Services Inc.
1555 Jarvis Crescent
Edmonton AB, T6L 6S3
Tel: 780-918-1143
Fax: 780-463-5841
eberhart@tsuga.ca

Enzoe, Peter
Lutsel K'e First Nation
Box 28
Lutsel K'e NT, X0E 1A0
Tel: 867-370-3197
wildlife@lutselke.com

Ewins, Peter J.
Director, Arctic Conservation
WWF-Canada
245 Eglington Avenue East, Suite
410
Toronto ON, M4P 3J1
Tel: 416-484-7711
Fax: 416-489-3611
pewins@wwfcanada.org

Festa-Bianchet, Marco
Département de biologic
Université de Sherbrooke
Sherbrooke, QC, J1R 2R1
Tel: 819-821-8000
Fax: 819-821-8049
marco.festa-
bianchet@usherbrooke.ca

Foote, Lee
Department of Renewable
Resources
University of Alberta
Edmonton AB, T6G 2P5
Tel: 780-492-4020
Fax: 780-492-4323
lee.foote@ualberta.ca

Freeman, Milton
Canadian Circumpolar Institute
University of Alberta
Edmonton AB, T6G 0H1
Tel: 780-492-4682
Fax:: 780-492-1153
milton.freeman@ualberta.ca

Gibson, Nancy
Science Director
Canadian Circumpolar Institute
University of Alberta
Edmonton AB, T6G 0H1
Tel: 780-492-3883
Fax: 780-492-1153
nancy.gibson@ualberta.ca

Giroux, J.R.
Alberta Conservation Association
P.O. Box 40027
Baker Centre Postal Outlet
Edmonton AB, T5J 4M9
Tel: 780-427-5192
Fax: 780-422-6441

Gissing, Drikus
Baffin Regional Manager
Wildlife Division
Department of Environment
Government of Nunavut
Box 446
Pond Inlet NU, X0A 0S0
Tel: 867-899-8034

Fax: 867-899-8711
dgissing@gov.nu.ca

Guthrie, Glen
Sahtu Renewable Resources
Board
Box 134
Tulita NT, X0E 0K0
Tel: 867-588-4040
Fax: 867-588-3324
rrco@srrb.nt.ca

Heikkila, Jari
Gwich'in Renewable Resources
Board
Box 2240
Inuvik NT, X0E 0T0
Tel: 867-777-6602
Fax: 867-777-6601
jari.heikkila@grrb.nt.ca

Hickey, Cliff
Research Area Leader
Sustainable Forestry
Management Network
University of Alberta
Edmonton AB, T6G 2E9
Tel: 780-492-1716
Fax: 780-492-8160
cliff.hickey@ualberta.ca

Hik, David
Department of Biological
Sciences
University of Alberta
Edmonton AB, T6G 2E9
Tel: 780-492-5570
Fax: 780-492-9234
dhik@ualberta.ca

Hudson, Robert
Department of Renewable
Resources
University of Alberta
Edmonton AB, T6G 2P5
Tel: 780-492-2111
Fax: 780-492-4323
robert.hudson@ualberta.ca

Hudson, Velma
Alberta Conservation Association
P.O. Box 40027
Baker Centre Postal Outlet
Edmonton AB, T5J 4M9
Tel: 780-427-5192
Fax: 780-422-6441

Hull, Steven
Alberta Conservation Association
P.O. Box 40027
Baker Centre Postal Outlet
Edmonton AB, T5J 4M9
Tel: 780-427-5192
Fax: 780-422-6441

Hutton, Jon
Chair, IUCN Sustainable Use
Specialist Group
Fauna & Flora International
Great Eastern House
Tenison Road
Cambridge CB1 2TT, U.K.
Tel: 44-7703-262434
jon.hutton@fauna-flora.org

Ikkidluak, Joannie
Chairman, Qikiqtaaluk Wildlife
Board Box 12
Kimmirut, NU, X0A 0N0
Tel: 867-939-2284
Fax: 867-939-2434
tdemcheson@nwmb.com

Inuktalik, Donald
Wildlife Management Advisory
Council (NWT)
Box 2120
Inuvik NT, X0E 0T0
Tel: 867-777-2828
Fax: 867-777-2610
wmacnwt@jointsec.nt.ca

Irngaut, Paul
Wildlife Department
Nunavut Tunngavik Inc.
Box 638
Iqaluit NU, X0A 0H0
irngaut@tunngavik.com

Jackson III, John J.
Conservation Force
3900 N. Causeway Blvd
Metairie, LA 70002
Tel: 504-837-1233
Fax: 504-837-1145
jjw-no@worldnet.att.net

Jaeb, Gary
True North Safaris Ltd.
3919 School Draw Avenue
Yellowknife NT, X1A 2J7
Tel: 867-873-8533
Fax: 867-920-4834
tnsafari@internorth.com

Kadlun, Phillip
Chairman
Kitikmeot Hunters & Trappers
Association
Box 309
Kugluktuk NU, X0B 1K0
Tel: 867-982-4207
Fax: 867-982-4047
agnes@polarnet.ca

Kiviaq
#300 Wentworth Bldg
10209 – 97 Street
Edmonton AB, T5J 0L6
Tel: 780-421-1059
Fax:: 780-429-2615
kiviaq@interbaun.com

Knopff, Kyle
Department of Biological
Sciences
University of Alberta
Edmonton AB, T6G 2E9
Tel: 780-492-6267
kknopff@ualberta.ca

Krogman, Naomi
Department of Rural Economy
University of Alberta
Edmonton AB, T6G 2P5
Tel: 780-492-4178
Fax: 780-4920268
naomi.krogman@ualberta.ca

Kublick, Darryl
Alberta Conservation
Association
P.O. Box 40027
Baker Centre Postal Outlet
Edmonton AB, T5J 4M9
Tel: 780-427-5192
Fax: 780-422-6441

Luckert, Marty
Department of Rural Economy
University of Alberta
Edmonton AB, T6G 2P5
Tel: 780-492-5002
Fax: 780-492-0268
marty.luckert@ualberta.ca

Mahoney, Shane P.
Executive Director
Science & Strategic Studies
Department of Environment
Government of Newfoundland &
Labrador
P.O. Box 8700
St. John's NF, A1B 4J6
Tel: 709-754-4780
conservationvisions@nl.rogers.com

Makpah, Ann
Nunavut Tunngavik Inc.
Box 280
Rankin Inlet NU, X0C 0G0
Tel: 867-645-5421
Fax: 867-645-3451
amakpah@arctic.ca

Maloney, Elaine L.
Assistant Director
Canadian Circumpolar Institute
University of Alberta
Edmonton AB, T6G 0H1
Tel: 780-492-4999
Fax: 780-492-1153
elaine.maloney@ualberta.ca

Mason, Cindy
Canadian Circumpolar Institute
University of Alberta
Edmonton AB, T6G 0H1
Tel: 780-492-4512
Fax: 780-492-1153
cindy.mason@ualberta.ca

Maurice, Jeff
Fisheries Advisor
Nunavut Tunngavik Inc.
Box 638
Iqaluit NU, X0A 0H0
Tel: 867-975-4900
Fax: 867-975-4949
maurice@tunngavik.com

McKinney, Ross
Chief Executive Officer
Game Council of New South
Wales
P.O. Box 2506
Orange, NSW 2800, Australia
Tel: 61-2-6360-5100
Fax: 61-2-6361-2093
ceo@gamecouncil.nsw.gov.au

Mullen, Shevenell
University of Alberta
9119 77 Avenue
Edmonton AB, T6C 0Mi
Tel: 780-452-9037
smmullen@ualberta.ca

Ningeocheak, Raymond
2nd Vice-President
Nunavut Tunngavik Inc.
Box 280
Rankin Inlet NU, X0C 0G0
Tel: 867-645-5405
Fax: 867-645-2609
raymondn@arctic.ca

Nirlungayuk, Gabriel
Director of Wildlife
Nunavut Tunngavik Inc.
Box 280
Rankin Inlet NU, X0C 0G0
Tel: 867-645-5435
Fax: 867-645-3451
gabnir@tunngavik.com

Norwegian, Herb
Grand Chief of the Deh Cho First
Nations
P.O. Box 89
Fort Simpson NT, X0E 0N0
Tel: 867-695-2355
herb_norwegian@dehchofirstnations.
com

Nuttall, Mark
Henry M. Tory Professor
Department of Anthropology
University of Alberta
Edmonton AB, T6G 2H4
Tel: 780-492-0129
Fax: 780-492-5273
mark.nuttall@ualberta.ca

Perry, Nelson
Inuvialuit Game Council
Box 2120
Inuvik NT, X0E 0T0
Tel: 867-777-2828
Fax: 867-777-2610
igc-js@jointsec.nt.ca

Pokiak, Frank
Chairman
Inuvialuit Game Council
Box 2120
Inuvik NT, X0E 0T0
Tel: 867-777-2828
Fax: 867-777-2610

Pokiak, James
Ookpik Tours & Adventures
Box 131
Tuktoyaktuk NT, X0E 1C0
Tel: 867-977-2170
Fax: 867-977-2399
jmpokiak@permafrost.com

Pokiak, Maureen
Ookpik Tours & Adventures
Box 131
Tuktoyaktuk NT, X0E 1C0
Tel: 867-977-2170
Fax: 867-977-2399
jmpokiak@permafrost.com

Potter, Jim
Alberta Conservation Association
P.O. Box 40027
Baker Centre Postal Outlet
Edmonton AB, T5J 4M9
Tel: 780-427-5192
Fax: 780-422-6441

Rabesca, Joyce
Tli Cho Outfitters
Camp Ekwo
Box 309
Rae NT, X0E 0Y0
Tel: 867-371-3144
Fax: 867-371-3155
campekwo@tamarack.nt.ca

Rabesca, Moise
Tli Cho Outfitters
Camp Ekwo
Box 309
Rae NT, X0E 0Y0
Tel: 867-371-3144
Fax: 867-371-3155
campekwo@tamarack.nt.ca

Rausch, Jennie
Earth & Atmospheric Sciences
University of Alberta
607-10711 Sask. Drive
Edmonton AB, T6E 4S4
Tel: 780-432-7904
jrausch@ualberta.ca

Ruben, Ruben
Inuvialuit Game Council
Box 2120
Inuvik NT, X0E 0T0
Tel: 867-777-2828
Fax: 867-777-2610
igc-js@jointsec.net.ca

Russell, Richard
Coordinator
Aboriginal Affairs and
Transboundary Wildlife Division
Canadian Wildlife Service
Gatineau QC, K1A 0H3
Tel: 819-997-1565
dick.russell@ec.gc.ca

Ruttan, Robert
Ruttan Consulting
Box 42, RR2
Tawatinaw AB, T0G 2E0
Tel: 780-698-2401
rsruttan@telusplanet.net

Salomons, Mike
Canadian Circumpolar Institute
University of Alberta
Edmonton AB, T6G 0H1
Tel: 867-492-0041
Fax: 867-492-1153
maguy@telusplanet.net

Samuel, Bill
ACCRU University of Alberta
Edmonton AB, T6G 2E9
Tel: 780-492-2360
Fax: 867-492-9234
bill.samuel@ualberta.ca

Schramm, Tanja
University of Alberta
Box 38, Site 260 RR2
Stony Plain AB, T7Z 1X2
Tel: 780-968-6389
tschramm@ualberta.ca

Scrimgeour, Garry
Alberta Conservation Association
P.O. Box 40027
Baker Centre Postal Outlet
Edmonton AB, T5J 4M9
Tel: 780-427-5192
Fax: 780-422-6441

Semple, Kelly
Executive Director
Hunting for Tomorrow
Foundation
#87, 4003-98th Street
Edmonton AB, T6E 6M8
Tel: 780-462-2444
Fax: 780-431-2871
ksemple@huntingfortomorrow.com

Smith, Barney
Fish & Wildlife Branch
Government of Yukon
P.O. Box 2703
Whitehorse YK, Y1A 2C6
Tel: 867-667-5767
Fax: 867-393-6405
barney.smith@gov.yk.ca

Smith, Harry
Yukon Fish & Wildlife
Management Board
Box 31104
Whitehorse, YK, Y1A 5P7
Tel: 867-667-3749
Fax: 867-393-6947
yfwmb@yknet.ca

Stevenson, Marc
Aboriginal & Northern Research
Manager
Sustainable Forestry
Management Network
University of Alberta
Edmonton AB, T6G 2E9
Tel: 780-492-2476
Fax: 780-492-8160
marc.stevenson@ualberta.ca

Taparti, Louis
Executive Assistant to 2nd Vice
President
Nunavut Tunngavik Inc.
Box 280
Rankin Inlet NU, X0C 0G0
Tel: 867-645-5400
Fax: 867-645-3451
ltaparti@arctic.ca

Thera, Trevor
Alberta Conservation Association
P.O. Box 40027
Baker Centre Postal Outlet
Edmonton AB, T5J 4M9
Tel: 780-427-5192
Fax: 780-422-6441

Turner, Robert
Northern Gas Project Secretariat
Suite 208, 5102 – 50 Avenue
Yellowknife NT, X1A 3S8
Tel: 867-766-8603
Fax: 867-766-8624
turner@ngps.nt.ca

Van Tighem, Graham
Yukon Fish & Wildlife
Management Board
Box 31104
Whitehorse, YK, Y1A 5P7
Tel: 867-667-3749
Fax: 867-393-6947
gvantighem@yknet.ca

Voaklander, Owen
Alberta Society of Professional
Outfitters
103 - 6030 88 Street
Edmonton AB, T6E 6G4
Tel: 780-414-0249
Fax: 780-465-6801
owen@apos.ab.ca

Wall, William A.
Conservation Biologist
14855 Purceville Road
Purceville, VA 20132
Tel: 540-668-6711
wawall900@earthlink.net

Webb, Jim
Little Red River Cree Nation
c/o SFMN
University of Alberta
Edmonton AB T6G 2E9
Fax: 780-492-8160
el2@ualberta.ca

Wenzel, George
Department of Geography
McGill University
805 Sherbrooke Street West
Montreal, QC, H3A 2K6
Tel: 514-398-4346
Fax: 514-398-7437
wenzel@geog.mcgill.ca

Williams, Glenn
Wildlife Advisor
Nunavut Tunngavik Inc.
Box 638
Iqaluit NU, X0A 0H0
Tel: 867-975-4900
Fax: 867-975-4949
glenwill@tunngavik.com

Wollscheid, Kai
Chief Executive Officer
CIC-International Council for
Game & Wildlife Conservation
P.O. Box 82
Budapest, H-2092, Hungary
Tel: 36-23-453-830
Fax: 36-23-453-832
k.wollscheid@cic-wildlife.org